Gender Dysphoria: Interdisciplinary Approaches in Clinical Management

Walter O. Bockting, Drs
Eli Coleman, PhD
Editors

The Haworth Press, Inc.
New York • London • Norwood (Australia)

Gender Dysphoria: Interdisciplinary Approaches in Clinical Management has also been published as *Journal of Psychology & Human Sexuality*, Volume 5, Number 4 1992.

The Haworth Press, Inc., 10 Alice Street, Binghamton, NY 13904-1580 USA

Library of Congress Cataloging-in-Publication Data

Gender dysphoria : interdisciplinary approaches in clinical management / Walter O. Bockting, Eli Coleman, editors.
    p. cm.
    ''Has also been published as Journal of psychology & human sexuality, volume 5, number 4, 1992''—T.p. verso.
    Includes bibliographical references.
    ISBN 1-56024-459-3 (h : alk. paper)—ISBN 1-56024-473-9 (pbk. : alk. paper)
    1. Gender identity disorders. I. Bockting, Walter O. II. Coleman, Eli.
    [DNLM: 1. Gender Identity. 2. Identification (Psychology) 3. Transsexualism—therapy. 4. Transsexualism—psychology. W1JO858B v. 5, no. 4 1992 / WM 610 G3254 1992]
RC560.G45G464 1992
616.85'83—dc20
DNLM/DLC
for Library of Congress
                                     93-20482
                                         CIP

This volume is dedicated to Paul Walker, Ph.D., and Robert J. Stoller, M.D., two experts who made critical contributions to the understanding and treatment of gender dysphoria. We thank Dr. Stoller for his in-depth psychoanalytic studies, and Dr. Walker for his far reaching compassion and care for the well being of our clients.

Gender Dysphoria: Interdisciplinary Approaches in Clinical Management

Gender Dysphoria: Interdisciplinary Approaches in Clinical Management

CONTENTS

∞   ALL HAWORTH BOOKS & JOURNALS
    ARE PRINTED ON CERTIFIED
    ACID-FREE PAPER

ABOUT THE EDITORS

Walter O. Bockting, Drs, is Instructor and Coordinator of the Gender Dysphoria Program at the Program in Human Sexuality, Department of Family Practice and Community Health, Medical School, University of Minnesota. Drs. Bockting began treating gender dysphoric clients at the Department of Clinical Psychology & Health, University of Utrecht, The Netherlands. After graduation from the Clinical Psychology Department of the Free University in Amsterdam, The Netherlands, he completed a Post-Doctoral Clinical/ Research Fellowship at the Program in Human Sexuality. Drs. Bockting has presented at many national and international conferences on his clinical work and research in the area of gender dysphoria. He has co-authored publications on homosexual identity development in sex reassigned female-to-male transsexuals. Current research projects include studying obsessive/compulsive features of crossdressing and gender dysphoria, as well as evaluating the effectiveness of a HIV/AIDS prevention program for the transgender population.

Drs. Bockting is a member of the Dutch Society for Sexology, the Society for the Scientific Study of Sex, the Harry Benjamin International Gender Dysphoria Association, and the International Council of Psychologists. He has served on the Board of Consulting Editors of the Journal of Psychology and Human Sexuality since 1990.

Eli Coleman, PhD, is Director and Associate Professor in the Program in Human Sexuality, Department of Family Practice and Community Health, Medical School, University of Minnesota in Minneapolis. Dr. Coleman has published numerous articles on the topics of sexual orientation, gender dysphoria, clinical approaches to the treatment of bisexuality and homosexuality, chemical dependency and family intimacy, and the treatment of a variety of sexual disorders. He has edited several Haworth Press publications including: *Psychotherapy with Homosexual Men and Women: Integrated Identity Approaches for Clinical Practice, Chemical Dependency and Intimacy Dysfunction, John Money: A Tribute, and Sex Offender Treatment: Psychological and Medical Approaches.*

Dr. Coleman is a member of several sexological organizations including the Society for the Scientific Study of Sex, the International Academy for Sex Research, the American Association of Sex Educators, Counselors and Therapists, the Sex and Information Council of the United States, and the Harry Benjamin International Gender Dysphoria Association.

Dr. Coleman has been the Editor of the Journal of Psychology and Human Sexuality since its inaugural issue in 1988.

Preface

Twenty-six years after publication of Harry Benjamin's pioneering work *The Transsexual Phenomenon* (Benjamin, 1966), it is appropriate to review the current status of the clinical management of gender dysphoria, and to determine a direction for the future.

Paul Walker, Ph.D., and Robert J. Stoller, M.D., two clinicians and researchers who devoted their careers to serving the gender dysphoric population, died in 1991. A new generation of experts is needed to continue the study and treatment of this complex phenomenon. In our educational activities we have encountered a growing interest among professionals and students in gender dysphoria and its implications for theories of sexual identity development and sexual health care. New developments in clinical sexology and a growing interdisciplinary approach to treatment have set the stage for a deeper understanding of the intense discomfort gender dysphoric clients endure. These advances also have indicated new avenues for treatment.

We invited an international pool of clinicians and researchers specialized in the area of gender identity disorders to submit contributions on their current treatment approaches. The result is this special volume, with a selection of eight articles.

Ira Pauly, whose publications on the clinical management of gender dysphoria go back to 1965, opens the collection with a review of terminology and classification of gender identity disorders, and a discussion of the current controversies over the proposed classification for DSM-IV. Given his central role in the conceptualization and treatment of gender dysphoria, Dr. Pauly presents an authoritative perspective on the evolution of the field.

The second paper, by Docter and Fleming, reports on the validation and factorial structure of the Cross-Gender Questionnaire developed by Richard Docter (author of *Transvestites and Transsexuals* (Docter, 1988)) and James Fleming. This instrument is an attempt to operationalize and measure the construct of cross-gen-derism as an alternative to gender dysphoria, the latter term being an ill-defined and loosely applied construct, according to the authors. Docter and Fleming recommend that theories of cross-gender phenom-ena be linked to mainstream psychological theory, and that until more systematic data are available, simplistic and incomplete diagnostic formulations be put aside. Such empirical testing of our theoretical concepts is critically important to the evolution of our field.

The two following papers from our Dutch colleagues discuss hor-mone treatment in gender dysphoric individuals undergoing anatomi-cal sex reassignment. Based on their extensive work with both male-to-female and female-to-male transsexuals, Henk Asscheman and Louis Gooren provide a much needed update on types of hormone therapy and the physical results they produce. Peggy Cohen-Kettenis and Louis Gooren review research on the effects of hormone treatment on the psychological functioning and mood of transsexuals, and con-clude that more systematic studies of these effects are needed.

Using data drawn from follow-up studies, as well as his own data from a large sample of sex-reassigned transsexuals, Friedemann Pfäfflin from Germany discusses transsexuals' reported regrets about surgery. His findings support the need for thorough assessment and psychotherapy to determine whether sex reassignment will aid in stabilizing the gender dysphoric client.

Dr. Leslie Lothstein, author of *Female-to-Male Transsexualism* (Lothstein, 1983) discusses genital mutilation in gender dysphoric young boys in his contribution. As in his earlier work, Lothstein emphasizes the often ignored affective component of gender dys-phoria, and recommends that reference to genital dysphoria be in-cluded in DSM IV classification.

An innovative model of female gender disorder is presented by Canadian sexologist Jeremy Baumbach and his American colleague Louisa Turner. This model, which distinguishes gender dysphoria from the fantasized solution of wishing to be the other sex and the request for anatomical sex reassignment, provides a diagnostic framework structuring the various clinical presentations of gender identity disor-ders. This article forms a resource for any clinician working with the under-researched subgroup of gender dysphoric females.

We complete this special publication with a description of a comprehensive treatment model we have developed and implemented over the past three years at the Gender Dysphoria Program of the University of Minnesota's Program in Human Sexuality. This model accounts for a wide spectrum of presentations of gender dysphoria. We emphasize that gender identity disorder needs to be understood and treated in the context of the client's overall psychosociosexual development.

Taken together, this collection of articles on the clinical management of gender dysphoria reflects the current status of this still young and specialized field. The discussions indicate that more theoretical development and research, both qualitatively and quantitatively, is needed to increase the understanding of the complex phenomena subsumed under the umbrella term gender dysphoria, as well as to improve the quality of clinical service to gender dysphoric clients.

The authors in this volume discuss the diverse presentations of gender dysphoria and its relations to other aspects of physical and psychosociosexual adjustment. The authors challenge the status quo of treatment approaches. Existing conceptualizations of gender identity disorders are criticized for their simplicity and limited applicability. A number of the articles in this special collection suggest changes in DSM classification. An approach to assessment and treatment that considers the overall physical and mental health care of the gender dysphoric client and results in a differential diagnosis and individualized treatment plan is advocated.

In the context of a growing political movement in transgender communities across North America and Europe arguing for a depathologization of cross-gender behavior (including removal of transvestism and transsexualism from DSM classification), the task of the clinician remains to provide up-to-date health care and ongoing support for gender dysphoric clients. This includes, but is not limited to, providing professional consultation regarding sex reassignment procedures. An interdisciplinary approach to treatment, research and education is essential for continuing progress.

May these writings inspire new and established clinicians and researchers to contribute to the further development of this field.

Walter O. Bockting, Drs, and Eli Coleman, PhD
Editors

REFERENCES

Benjamin, H. (1966). *The transsexual phenomenon*. New York: The Julian Press, Inc.

Docter, R. (1988). *Transvestites and transsexuals*. New York: The Plenum Press.

Lothstein, L. (1983). *Female-to-male transsexualism*. Boston: Routledge & Kegan Paul.

Terminology and Classification of Gender Identity Disorders

Ira B. Pauly, MD

SUMMARY. German clinicians began describing individuals with some form of gender discomfort over 160 years ago. This culminated with the publication of *Die Transvestiten* by Magnus Hirschfeld in 1910. Currently, the most commonly used terms for these conditions are transsexualism, gender dysphoria, and gender identity disorders (GID). With the publication of the 3rd edition of The Diagnostic and Statistical Manual (DSM-III) of the American Psychiatric Association in 1980, one finds mention of these GID for the first time in a formal diagnostic classification system. These GID were further legitimized in 1987, with the publication of DSM-III-Revised. Currently, DSM-IV is under preparation by a subcommittee on GID. There is considerable controversy about revisions in terminology and classification of these GID currently under discussion. This paper also deals with the relationship between gender identity and sexual orientation. There is some evidence to suggest a correlation between age of onset of gender dysphoria and sexual orientation subsequently established. Finally, the author discusses the pros and cons of a recommendation to remove GID from DSM-IV altogether. Those in favor of such a recommendation argue that their inclusion stigmatizes gender dysphoric individuals by placing a psychiatric label on them.

INTRODUCTION

The concept of cross-gender identity and behavior has been known since antiquity (Pauly, 1965; 1968; 1969a, 1969b; Green and Money, 1969). However, it was not until the early 19th century

---

Ira B. Pauly is Professor and Chairman, Department of Psychiatry and Behavioral Sciences, University of Nevada School of Medicine, Reno, NV 89557-0046.

that this condition was first described in the medical literature (Friedreich, 1830). Subsequent German sexologists continued to describe examples of cross-gender behavior, using terms like "the contrary sexual feeling" (Westphal, 1869), and "metamorphosis sexualis paranoia" (Krafft-Ebing, 1877). This German tradition culminated with the work of Magnus Hirschfeld and the publication of his classic monograph *Die Transvestiten* (1910). The term transvestism was translated into the English literature, and was widely used to describe cases of gender dysphoria. Havelock Ellis coined the terms "sexoesthetic inversion" and "eonism" to describe this condition (Ellis, 1936). D.O. Caldwell first used the term "transsexualism" in 1949, and it has been used ever since to describe the most extreme examples of gender dysphoria. However, it was not until the famous Christine Jorgensen case received world-wide attention in the press that transsexualism became known to the public and medical field. Harry Benjamin, an endocrinologist and sexologist from New York, popularized the term "transsexualism" in his writing (Benjamin, 1953) which culminated with the publication of his classic monograph *The Transsexual Phenomenon* (Benjamin, 1966). Dr. Benjamin was recognized for his leadership and pioneering work in this field by having the International Gender Dysphoria Association named after him. In 1974, the term "gender dysphoria" was coined, and this has become a generic term that includes all individuals who suffer from some form of gender discomfort (Fisk, 1974; and Laub and Fisk, 1974). Finally, the term "gender identity disorders" (GID) has been used to describe individuals with gender dysphoria since 1980 with the publication of DSM-III, and this generic term continues to be the primary designation for this group of disorders.

THE CLASSIFICATION OF GID IN THE DIAGNOSTIC AND STATISTICAL MANUAL (DSM)

In 1980, the American Psychiatric Association published the third edition of its *Diagnostic and Statistical Manual of Mental Disorders* (American Psychiatric Association, 1980). Included in the category on psychosexual disorders was a section on gender identity disorders. Under this section was included the diagnostic criteria for GID/Children, Transsexualism; GID/Adolescent and Adult, Non-transsexual Type (GIDAANT); and GID/Not Otherwise Specified (GID/NOS). Each of the above diagnoses had its own code number. Transsexualism was further subtyped as homosexual, heterosexual, or asexual. Also included in this category on sexual disorders were the paraphilias, sexual dysfunctions, and other psychosexual disorders, including ego-dystonic homosexuality. The inclusion of these GID further legitimized these forms of gender dysphoria by formally recognizing them as conditions worthy of evaluation and treatment. In addition, insurance carriers now would be expected to pay for services rendered on behalf of such patients. Finally, sex reassignment surgery (SRS) was presented as a legitimate treatment and not simply elective, cosmetic surgery (Pauly, 1981; 1985; Pauly and Edgerton, 1986). Given the large readership of DSM, medical students, psychiatric residents, psychology interns and residents, as well as all the practicing disciplines within the broad mental health field, had simple and clear guidelines for making the correct diagnosis, which subsequently led them to refer these patients to the appropriate gender clinic or individual professional.

In 1987, the third edition of DSM was revised, currently referred to as DSM-III-R (American Psychiatric Association, 1987). In this revision there were further refinements within the section on gender identity disorders. The section on GID was removed from the category of sexual disorders and placed in the large section entitled "Disorders Usually First Evident in Infancy, Childhood, or Adolescence." Although appropriately placed in this category, GID were somewhat lost, since they had no place in the table of contents. One had to refer to the index and look up transsexualism, in order to find the appropriate listing. Also, some gender dysphoric individuals present themselves to clinicians as adults, and may or may not have had gender identity problems as children. These late-onset or secondary transsexuals are not easily diagnosed given the current classification system. The brief description of treatment for GID in DSM-III-R is very cursory and quite negative as to prognosis with hormone therapy and/or SRS. Finally, the subtyping of homosexual and heterosexual transsexuals was causing more problems than it was solving because it used as the reference point one's original biological or genetic sex, rather than one's gender identity or sexual anatomy after SRS (Coleman and Bockting, 1988; Pauly, 1990a, 1990b).

All of the above problems set the stage for the next revision of the DSM or DSM-IV. A work group was established by The American Psychiatric Association as a subcommittee on GID in March of 1989, and has worked hard to prepare the GID section in DSM-IV. It is anticipated that DSM-IV will come out in 1994. A preliminary or interim report of this subcommittee's work already has been published (Bradley, Coates, Green, Levine, Mayer-Bahlburg, Pauly, and Zucker, 1991). Several important issues are still under consideration. First and foremost, is the subcommittee's recommendation that gender identity disorders deserve a place of their own in DSM-IV, and should no longer be hidden in the section "Disorders Usually First Evident in Infancy, Childhood, or Adolescence." Like anxiety disorders and mood disorders, GID should be listed in the table of contents under its own name. This would not preclude a cross-reference to GID/Children in the section on childhood disorders, just as is done for anxiety or mood disorders. Certainly this independent placement would indicate that GID have become well established and accepted in the mainstream of modern psychiatry. However, it is not within the jurisdiction of the work group to insist upon this modification.

Of greatest significance in the recommendations by the work group is the decision to create a single, broad category of GID. This decision is predicated on the concern by some that the term transsexualism automatically carries with it a recommendation in favor of SRS (Levine, 1989). According to the interim report "Transsexualism appears designed for gender dysphoric individuals who have decided upon surgical sex reassignment as the solution to their inner distress" (Bradley et al., 1991). The interim report goes on to say, "The desire to uncouple the clinical diagnosis of gender dysphoria from criteria for approving patients for SRS was one factor in the subcommittee's recommendation that these categories be merged under the single heading of "GID." The author feels that the elimination of the term transsexualism is a serious mistake, especially since that term has been used in the literature for over 40 years and is a recognized clinical syndrome. The subcommittee's concern that the diagnosis transsexualism simply reflects the patient's perception that only SRS is the solution to his/her problem is not sufficient justification for removing this well-accepted term. Just because a patient comes in and states that he or she is depressed, does not mean that the clinician is going to make the diagnosis of major depression and prescribe an anti-depressant medication or electro-convulsive treatment. Either the patient meets the full criteria for the diagnosis or he/she does not. The real issue here is whether the gender dysphoric individual gives a clear-cut history of "persistent discomfort and sense of inappropriateness about one's assigned sex" and that he/she reports "persistent preoccupation for at least two years with getting rid of one's primary and secondary sex characteristics and acquiring the sex characteristics of the other sex" (American Psychiatric Association, 1987).

Making the diagnosis of transsexualism is *not* synonymous with the clinician recommending the person for sex-reassignment surgery (Pauly, 1990a, 1990b). The "Standards of Care" published by the HBIGDA make this very clear (Walker, Berger, Green, Laub, Reynolds, and Wollman, 1985): "Hormone treatment and/or SRS *on demand* is contra-indicated. It is herein declared to be professionally improper to perform hormonal sex reassignment or SRS without careful evaluation of the patient's reasons for requesting such services, and evaluation of the beliefs and attitudes upon which such reasons are based." Furthermore, the clinician, before recommending SRS must:

1. Have known the patient for at least six months before endorsing the patient's request for genital SRS.
2. Require the patient to be evaluated by another psychologist or psychiatrist, who will have recommended in favor of SRS. At least one of two must be a psychiatrist.
3. Require the patient to have lived *successfully* in the opposite gender role for at least one year.
4. Require the patient to have undergone a urological examination.

In spite of the above guidelines for recommending in favor of SRS, the majority of the subcommittee saw fit "to uncouple the clinical diagnosis of the gender dysphoria from criteria for approving patients for SRS" (Bradley, et al., 1991) by merging the DSM-III-R categories of GID/Childhood, Transsexualism and GIDAANT under the single heading of Gender Identity Disorder (GID). Thus, the term transsexualism will be removed from DSM-IV. The author, obviously representing a dissenting opinion against this decision, has tried to suggest a compromise to this position, wherein the term transsexualism could be preserved until the users of DSM-IV could be educated to the new terminology. I have suggested that each of the following categories have their own code number and diagnostic criteria: GID/Childhood, GID/Transsexual Type, GID/Non-transsexual Type, and GID/Not Otherwise Specified. Using this scheme, GID/Transsexual Type would preserve the criteria used for transsexualism in DSM-III-R and would obviously represent the most severe form of gender dysphoria. The treatment for GID/Transsexual Type would not automatically be SRS, but would depend on further evaluation according to the Standards of Care. GID/Non-transsexual Type would preserve the DSM-III-R criteria for GIDAANT and would describe a less severe example of gender dysphoria which is persistent, but does not aim at SRS. Finally, the term GID/NOS will be maintained in DSM-IV to include the least severe forms of gender dysphoria, in which the cross-gender identity and/or behavior is fluctuating and less persistent.

There was considerable discussion in the work group as to whether individuals who have undergone SRS should have a diagnostic category specified for them, i.e., GID/Post-surgery. Although this designation would distinguish between those individuals who had been diagnosed and treated with SRS from other gender dysphoric individuals, these individuals may no longer see themselves as requiring treatment. Thus, for political and other reasons, this post-surgical category will not be included in DSM-IV.

This compromise is currently under discussion. The author feels it is important to distinguish different levels of severity of GID, as well as to maintain some continuity with previous terminology. An important aspect of any classification system is to assist in the recommendation for the appropriate treatment of these disorders. Unless some connection with past terminology is maintained, specifically, unless the term transsexualism is continued in some manner in DSM-IV, I anticipate that much of what was gained for patients suffering from gender dysphoria with the publication of DSM-III and DSM-III-R will be lost in DSM-IV. Finally, the author believes that the term "transsexualism" will continue to be used by the clinician and in the medical literature, and confusion will arise if this terminology is not found in DSM-IV.

GID AND SEXUAL ORIENTATION

As mentioned previously, there was confusion and dissatisfaction with the subcategories of heterosexual, homosexual and asexual suggested in DSM-III and DSM-III-R (Coleman, Bockting, and Gooren, in press; Pauly, 1990c). Over the years, it has become clear that a significant percentage of gender dysphoric males have come forward to request SRS in order to live in the female role, and pursue a relationship with lesbian women. A post-operative male to female transsexual, now equipped with a neo-vagina, and her lesbian partner would be referred to as "heterosexual" in the current DSM-III-R terminology. In DSM-IV, the term heterosexual will be deleted and replaced with "sexually attracted to females," in the above example. The terms heterosexual or homosexual have as their reference the individual's original biological status, the anatomy of which could be changed, through SRS (Coleman and Bockting, 1988; Pauly, 1990c). Obviously, one's genetic status remains the same, in spite of hormone therapy or SRS. Nonetheless, the important variable is not the genetics of the relationship, but the gender status of the two participants. The author had previously suggested the terms heterogenderal to pertain to a male to female transsexual who relates to heterosexual men, and homogenderal as a descriptor for male to female transsexuals who relate to homosexual women as partners (Pauly, 1974). However, the same point is achieved, perhaps with less confusion or bias, by simply stating "sexually attracted to males, sexually attracted to females, sexually attracted to both, sexually attracted to neither, or unspecified."

The sexual orientation of gender dysphorics has become an important issue in distinguishing primary and secondary forms of gender dysphoria (Pauly, 1990c). Ray Blanchard of The Clark Institute of Toronto has analyzed the sexual orientation of gender dysphoric males applying to the Gender Identity Clinic of that institution (Blanchard, 1985; 1988, 1989a, and 1989b). He has argued that there are basically two types of gender dysphoric males, homosexual and non-homosexual, using the current DSM-III-R subtyping. The first and most common (55%) "homosexual" group are biological males who would have met the criteria for GID/Childhood as boys and go on to meet the criteria for Transsexualism as adults and are sexually attracted to heterosexual men (Blanchard, 1989b). This group would also be referred to as primary transsexuals, since their cross-gender identity existed from an early age. The second group, Blanchard labelled as "non-homosexual," and included heterosexual, bisexual, and asexual GID individuals. Collectively the second group represented some 45% of those gender dysphoric males who presented to the Clark Institute's Gender Identity Clinic. This group acknowledged a significant history of erotic arousal in association with cross-dressing (transvestism), were significantly older at initial presentation than the homosexual subjects, reported less childhood femininity, and were more likely to have been sexually aroused by the fantasy of having a woman's body (autogynephilia). This "non-homosexual" group, represents a secondary form of transsexualism and appears to be making a gender accommodation to their underlying ego-dystonic transvestism (Pauly, 1990c). This would begin to explain why their sexual orientation differs from the more common expectation of those whose gender dysphoria stem back to childhood. Green has demonstrated that most GID boys grow up to become homosexual men as adults (1987). Thus, there appears to be some evidence to suggest a correlation between the age of onset of gender dysphoria in boys and the sexual orientation subsequently established. Specifically, the earlier these boys established a feminine gender identity, the more likely they were to prefer men as sexual partners as adults. However, we know that many homosexual men are not, nor have they ever been effeminate. Thus, there is conflicting evidence as to the relationship between gender identity and sexual orientation. Are these independent or dependent variables (Pauly, 1990c)?

Thus far, I have focused on the male of the species, in discussing the relationship between gender identity and sexual orientation.

Very little literature exists on the subject of female to male trans-sexuals' preference for sexual partner. Originally, the author reported that all female to male transsexuals were sexually attracted to heterosexual women (Pauly, 1974). More recently, so called female to gay male transsexualism has been identified (Blanchard, Clemmensen, and Steiner, 1987; Coleman and Bockting, 1988; Coleman, Bockting, and Gooren, in press; Clare and Tully, 1989; Lothstein, 1983; Pauly, 1990c). Clare has used the term transhomosexuality to describe individuals whose sexual orientation and identification is with homosexual persons of the opposite biological sex (Clare and Tully, 1989). However, the numbers of such female to gay male transsexuals appear to be very small, 1 in 70 cases in one study (Blanchard et al., 1987). Most of the female to male transsexuals who would have met the criteria for GID/Childhood appear to develop a sexual orientation for heterosexual women (Pauly, 1974). However, the literature is beginning to reflect an increased incidence of female to male transsexuals who prefer gay men as sexual partners (Coleman, Bockting, and Gooren, in press; Pauly, 1990c). It is not yet established whether these female to male transsexual subjects who are sexually attracted to gay men will turn out to be secondary transsexuals, that is to say, who develop their gender dysphoria after first having established a feminine identity in childhood. Suffice it to say that the study of the sexual orientation of gender dysphoric and/or transsexual individuals has potential to shed light on the broader topic of sexual orientation. However, our understanding of the fundamental relationship between gender identity and sexual orientation is only beginning to emerge, and further research on GID promises to be fruitful.

A MOVEMENT TO REMOVE GID FROM DSM-IV

There is a movement afoot to remove GID from DSM altogether. Some advocate groups representing gender dysphoric individuals take the position that classifying this condition as a psychiatric disorder is stigmatizing these people by placing a psychiatric label on them. They take the position that gender dysphoria or GID are simply a normal variant of the human condition. Thus, they make the same point as advocates for removing homosexuality from DSM-III did in the mid-1970s. As the reader may recall, this effort to remove homosexuality from DSM-III was successful, after a long and bitter controversy. However, the author sees important differences in the justification for removing homosexuality from the DSM-III and the rationale for doing the same thing with transsexualism and/or GID in DSM-IV.

First, transsexualism is much rarer than homosexuality, thus it is more difficult to sustain an argument that these GID are simply a variation of the human condition. Secondly, a homosexual individual need not present to the medical or psychiatric profession in order to pursue his/her lifestyle. The exception to this might be the individual who is conflicted about his/her sexual orientation. The individual with GID requires evaluation by the psychiatric profession, so that appropriate referrals for hormone treatment and/or SRS can be separated from those individuals for whom this recommendation would be contra-indicated. Time has taught us the tragedy of approving SRS for individuals who were not carefully evaluated by the mental health profession. The Standards of Care published by the gender profession (Walker et al., 1985) clearly require a significant period of evaluation and observation in the gender of preference before recommending in favor of SRS or even hormone treatment. Since these procedures are clearly irreversible, it is entirely appropriate that a careful assessment be made by an experienced professional.

Another reason why homosexuality was deleted from DSM-III was because non-clinical samples of homosexuals demonstrated no more psychopathology than heterosexuals. Gender dysphoric individuals do have a significant incidence of mood disorders (Pauly, 1990a) as well as Axis II pathology (Levine, 1989). This is further justification for retaining GID in DSM-IV.

Last, but not least, is the very practical issue that unless a condition is classified as a disorder, the insurance carrier will not reimburse the individual for the cost of professional care. Important battles have already been waged and won for transsexuals whose medical, surgical, and psychiatric care have been paid by insurance carriers. Nonetheless, this issue will be raised by some who feel that the classification of GID in DSM-IV or DSM-V does stigmatize these individuals. Labels will be coined which are the gender equivalent of homophobia, and a political battle will ensue to rectify what some consider to be an injustice for these gender dysphoric individuals. Perhaps the most significant reason for retaining GID in the diagnostic classification system is the extent to which research in this field has been facilitated by having standardized criteria available for correctly diagnosing individuals with GID. This enables researchers to compare their findings on subjects with the same diagnosis. We are no longer comparing apples and oranges, but rather we are sharing research findings on comparable subjects. This has greatly increased our knowledge and understanding of GID, and has resulted in improved and more standardized treatment protocols (Walker et al., 1985). In the author's opinion, the inclusion of these conditions in the formal diagnostic classification system has solved more problems than it has created.

CONCLUSION

1. Beginning in 1830, German clinicians began describing individuals with gender dysphoria in the European literature. This culminated with the publication of *Die Transvestiten* by Magnus Hirschfeld in 1910. Terms such as transsexualism, gender dysphoria, and GID were defined, and are now in current usage to describe individuals who experience some form of gender discomfort.

2. In 1980, The American Psychiatric Association published its third edition of DSM, in which GID were listed for the first time. The next revision of DSM in 1987 refined this section. This has resulted in more widespread understanding, diagnosis, and appropriate treatment for GID individuals.

3. Currently, a subcommittee is addressing the next update for DSM-IV. A single, broad category of GID will incorporate the DSM-III-R designations of GID/Children, Transsexualism, GIDAANT. Unfortunately, the term "transsexualism" may be removed from DSM-IV as a specific diagnostic category.

4. More and more GID individuals are acknowledging and presenting with varying sexual orientation. A significant percentage of male to female transsexuals are opting for lesbian relationships, and

individual cases of female to gay male transsexualism have begun to emerge, although the percentage appears much less than with male to female transsexuals who are attracted to lesbian women.

5. The relationship between gender identity and sexual orientation has come under some investigation as the result of following GID individuals. There is some evidence to suggest a correlation between age of onset of gender dysphoria and sexual orientation subsequently established. However, an understanding of this fundamental biopsychosocial relationship is only beginning to emerge. Further research promises to be fruitful in clarifying this important relationship.

6. There appears to be a movement to remove GID from the psychiatric classification system altogether. Some claim that gender dysphoric individuals are stigmatized by having a psychiatric label placed on them without justification. Those who recommend the removal of GID from DSM-IV use as a precedent the removal of homosexuality from DSM-III. The author opposes this position.

REFERENCES

American Psychiatric Association. (1980). *Diagnostic and Statistical Manual of Mental Disorders* 3rd ed. A.P.A.: Washington, D.C.

American Psychiatric Association. (1987). *Diagnostic and Statistical Manual of Mental Disorders* 3rd ed., revised. A.P.A.: Washington, D.C.

Benjamin, H. (1953). Transvestism and transsexualism. *International Journal of Sexology*, 7, 12-14.

Benjamin, H. (1966). *The Transsexual Phenomenon*. Julian Press: New York.

Blanchard, R. (1985). Typology of male-to-female transsexualism. *Archives of Sexual Behavior*, 14, 247-261.

Blanchard, R. (1988). Nonhomosexual gender dysphoria. *Journal of Sexual Research*, 24, 188-193.

Blanchard, R. (1989a). The classification and labeling of nonhomosexual gender dysphorias. *Archives of Sexual Behavior*, 18, 315-334.

Blanchard, R. (1989b). The concept of autogynephilia and the typology of male gender dysphoria. *Journal of Nervous and Mental Disorders*, 177, 616-623.

Blanchard, R., Clemmensen, L., & Steiner, B. (1987). Heterosexual and homosexual gender dysphoria. *Archives of Sexual Behavior*, 16, 139-152.

Bradley, S., Blanchard, R., Coates, S., Green, R., Levine, S., Meyer-Bahlburg, H., Pauly, I., & Zucker, K. (1991). Interim report of the DSM-IV subcommittee on gender identity disorders. *Archives of Sexual Behavior*, 20, 333-343.

Cauldwell, D.O. (1949). Psychopathia transsexualis. *Sexology*, 16, 274-280.

Clare, D. & Tully, B. (1989). Transhomosexuality, or the Dissociation of Sexual Orientation and Sex Object Choice. *Archives of Sexual Behavior*, 18, 531-536.

Coleman, E. & Bockting, W. (1988). Heterosexual prior to sex reassignment–Homosexual afterwards: A case study of a female-to-male transsexual. *Journal of Psychology and Human Sexuality*, 12, 69-82.

Coleman, E., Bockting, W., & Gooren, L. (in press). Homosexual and bisexual identity in sex-reassigned female-to-male transsexuals. *Archives of Sexual Behavior*, in press.

Ellis, H. (1936). Eonism. *Studies in Psychology of Sex*. New York: Random House, 2, 1-110.

Fisk, N. (1974). Gender dysphoria syndrome. In D. Laub & P. Gandy (Eds.) *Proceedings of the Second Interdisciplinary Symposium on Gender Dysphoria Syndrome*. Ann Harbor: Edwards Brothers, 7-14.

Friedreich, J. (1830). *Versuch Einer Literargeschichte der Pathologie und Therapie der psychischen Krankheiten*. Würzburg.

Green, R. (1987). *The Sissy Boy Syndrome*. New Haven: Yale University Press.

Green R. & Money, J. (Eds.) (1969). *Transsexualism and Sex Reassignment*. Baltimore: The Johns Hopkins Press.

Hirschfeld, M. (1910). *Die Transvestiten*. Leipzig: Max Spohr.

Krafft-Ebing, R. (1877). Über Gewisse Anomalien des Geschlechtstriebes. *Archiven für Psychiatrie und Nervenkrankheiten*, 7, 291-312.

Laub, D. & Fisk, N. (1974). A rehabilitation program for gender dysphoria syndrome by surgical sex change. *Plastic & Reconstructive Surgery*, 53, 388-403.

Levine, S. (1989). Gender identity disorders of childhood, adolescence, and adulthood. In H. Kaplan, & B. Sadock (Eds.) *Comprehensive Textbook of Psychiatry*. Vol. I, 5th Ed., Baltimore: Williams and Wilkins, 1061-1069.

Lothstein, L. (1983). *Female-to-Male Transsexualism*. Boston: Routledge and Kegan Paul.

Pauly, I. (1965). Male psychosexual inversion: Transsexualism. *Archives of General Psychiatry*, 13, 172-181.

Pauly, I. (1968). The current status of the change of sex operation. *Journal of Nervous Mental Disorders*, 147, 460-471.

Pauly, I. (1969a). Adult manifestations of male transsexualism. In R. Green & J. Money (Eds.). *Transsexualism and Sex Reassignment*. Baltimore: Johns Hopkins University Press, 37-58.

Pauly, I. (1969b). Adult manifestations of female transsexualism. In R. Green & J. Money (Eds.) *Transsexualism and Sex Reassignment*. Baltimore: Johns Hopkins University Press, 59-87.

Pauly, I. (1974). Female transsexualism, Parts I & II. *Archives of Sexual Behavior*, 3, 487-525.

Pauly, I. (1981). Outcome of sex reassignment surgery for transsexuals. *Australia & New Zealand Journal of Psychiatry*, 15, 45-51.

Pauly, I. (1985). Gender identity disorders. In M. Farber (Ed.) *Textbook of Human Sexuality*, New York: Macmillan Pub. Co., 295-316.

Pauly, I. (1990a). Gender Identity Disorders: Evaluation and Treatment. *Journal of Sex Education & Therapy*, 16, 2-24.

Pauly, I. (1990b). Gender identity disorders: Update. In F.J. Bianco & R.H. Serrano (Eds.) *Sexology: An Independent Field*. Amsterdam: Elsevier, 63-84.

Pauly, I. (1990c). Gender identity and sexual preference: Dependent versus independent variables. In F.J. Bianco & R.H. Serrano (Eds.) *Sexology: An Independent Field*. Amsterdam: Elsevier, 51-62.

Pauly, I. & Edgerton, M. (1986). The gender identity movement: A growing surgical-psychiatric liaison. *Archives of Sexual Behavior*, 15, 315-329.

Walker, P., Berger, J., Green, R., Laub, D., Reynolds, C., & Wollman, L. (1985). Standards of care: The hormonal and surgical sex reassignment of gender dysphoric persons. *Archives of Sexual Behavior*, 14: 79-90.

Westphal, C. (1869). Die konträre sexualempfindung. *Archiven Für Psychiatrie und Nervenkrankheiten*, 11, 73-108.

Dimensions
of Transvestism and Transsexualism:
The Validation and Factorial Structure
of the Cross-Gender Questionnaire

Richard F. Docter, PhD
James S. Fleming, PhD

SUMMARY. A 55 item questionnaire was developed to assess cross-genderism in adult males. The subjects were a nonclinical sample of 518 self-described heterosexual transvestites, 78 marginal transvestites ("borderline transsexuals"), and 86 transsexuals living full-time as women. Using factor analyses, several hypotheses were tested concerning the factorial structure of cross-genderism. The best solution was a model wherein cross-genderism was seen as consisting of four correlated but independent factors: Cross-gender Identity, Cross-gender Feminization, Cross-gender Social/Sexual Role, and Cross-gender Sexual Arousal. Procedurally, 692 subjects were randomly divided into validation and cross-validation samples of equal size. A series of exploratory analyses and item selection processes

---

Richard F. Docter is Chair and Professor of Psychology and James S. Fleming is Lecturer in Psychology, both at California State University, Northridge.

Address correspondence to: Richard F. Docter, PhD, Department of Psychology, CSUN, Northridge, CA 91330.

Authors' Note: The support of the Research and Grants Office, California State University, Northridge is gratefully acknowledged; we're also very appreciative for support provided by the CSUN Department of Psychology and the Computer Center. We thank our colleagues in the Department of Psychology for their assistance and suggestions. Much of the data input and management of feedback reports to our subjects was handled by Denise Edmiston. The Renaissance Education Association was very helpful with the distribution of our questionnaire; many other groups also assisted us and we thank each of them. We are especially grateful to the 692 individuals who have shown their confidence in us by participating in this long-term project.

15

was followed by a replication using the cross-validation sample; the replication results were nearly identical. Scale reliabilities were satisfactory as were three tests of goodness-of-fit for the four factor solution. Partial validation evidence was based on analyses of variance showing that each of the four factor means scores differs significantly across three self-reported levels of cross-genderism (transvestites, marginal transvestites, and transsexuals).

This report describes a 55 item questionnaire measure of cross-genderism applicable to adult male transvestites and male-to-female transsexuals. We define this construct as the propensity for nonconforming gender cognition and behavior. While cross-genderism occurs in both men and women our studies are restricted to biological males. At one end of the continuum, cross-genderism may be experienced as pleasant fantasies or identifications which are not acted upon (e.g., a male who merely fantasizes, "I wish I had been born a woman"). At the other extreme, cross-genderism is exemplified by the male who prefers to live her/his life continuously in the role of a woman. Spanning the middle range of cross-genderism are episodic transvestite males, many of whom report cross-gender feelings said to be strongest during periods when they are cross-dressed and portraying a woman. Using factor analyses and other psychometric procedures, we test a series of hypotheses concerning the factorial structure of cross-genderism and provide partial validation, reliabilities, and goodness-of-fit results pertaining to the identified factors.

MEASURES OF CROSS-GENDERISM AND GENDER DYSPHORIA

Freund (1985) and his colleagues at the University of Toronto's Clarke Institute of Psychiatry have taken leadership in the conceptualization and measurement of cross-gender identity (Blanchard, 1985a,b; Freund, Nagler, Langevin, Zajac, & Steiner, 1974; Freund, Langevin, Satterberg, & Steiner, 1977; Freund, Steiner, & Chan, 1982; Freund, Watson, & Dickey, 1991). Langevin, Marjpruz, and Handy (1990) evaluated the Gender Dysphoria scale developed by

Althof, Lothstein, Jones, and Shen (1983). Based on items from the Minnesota Multiphasic Personality Inventory, this scale differentiated between diagnostically different groups of gender dysphoric subjects. However, it failed to separate so-called gender dysphoric subjects from non-gender dysphoric homosexual males. Additionally, the internal reliability proved low and it was reported to be "biased" relative to education and intelligence.

Freund defines cross-gender identity as ". . . a physically mature person's wish or wishful fantasy that his or her body had the shape typical for the opposite gender." Continuing, he writes, "Cross-gender identity is always associated with further cognitive patterns or behaviors seen by the individual as characteristic of the opposite gender . . ." (1985, pp. 259-260). Freund's 1974 report described the development of measures to differentiate males on the basis of erotic preference and gender identity. In 1977 he reported an extended Gender Identity Scale consisting of 29 questionnaire items. In a later report Freund, Steiner, and Chan (1982) used the Freund Gender Identity Questionnaire in their typological studies of transvestites and transsexuals. Working with males, they identified two types of cross-gender identity, one characteristic of heterosexuals and the second seen in homosexual males. A life-long history of intense cross-gender identity was seen in homosexuals who became transsexuals, but not in heterosexuals who made this change. They also noted an intermediate group of so-called marginal transvestites or borderline transsexuals.

Building upon the work of Freund, Steiner, and Chan (1982), Blanchard (1985b) described three variables believed most critical in the assessment of transvestites and transsexuals: (a) Periodicity of cross-gender identity, (b) erotic partner preference, and (c) cross-gender fetishism. In additional studies Blanchard (1989a,b) again used items and scales which had, in part, been employed by Freund and his associates. Using a sample of men identified as gender dysphoric, Blanchard reported three factors tapped by his measures: (a) Core Autogynephilia, which refers to sexual arousal from the fantasy of being a woman without any actual interpersonal exchange, (b) Autogynephilic Interpersonal Fantasy, which refers to the sexual fantasy of being admired in the female persona by another person, and (c) Alloeroticism, which refers to the dimension of sexual attraction versus indifference toward other persons.

As reviewed above, several previous investigators have described self-report questionnaires which successfully differentiated among groups of so-called gender dysphoric men. But the focus of these studies has typically been upon typological issues and not scale development or measurement of constructs. Existing scales seem to us to contain too few items to assess the variables of concern at several levels of behavioral expression, ranging from fantasy and plans through overt behavior. Judging from previous reports, the variables which seem most important in the assessment of transvestites and transsexuals are cross-gender identity and cross-gender sexual arousal. Finishing third would be homoerotic orientation, a variable which is often unclear in the thinking of gender distressed men, and which did not discriminate among gender identity disordered males (Freund, Watson, & Dickey, 1991). While we are also interested in the part erotic orientation may play in cross-genderism, this is not one of the focal concerns of the present report.

We began with the assumption that our data set would yield one of these factorial solutions: (a) A single factor, possibly cross-gender identity, which would tap a high percentage of the variance; (b) A two-factor solution possibly consisting of cross-gender identity and cross-gender sexual arousal; (c) A multi-factor model based on three or more variables. We also sought to replicate both our item selection process and the exploratory factor analysis from a cross-validation sample. Additionally, we sought to determine if the measure or measures of cross-genderism under development here would yield significantly different mean scores across groups of self-described transvestites, marginal transvestites (borderline transsexuals) and transsexuals.

METHOD

Development of the Cross-Genderism Questionnaire

Data Collection and Sample of Subjects

Beginning in October, 1990 a 113 item questionnaire was distributed nationwide through support groups of transsexuals and transvestites. A "snowball" sample was acquired through the cooperation of many of our subjects and the clubs to which they belonged. One nationally distributed newsletter (Renaissance News, 1991) printed the entire questionnaire and invited their subscribers to respond. The questionnaire was described and distributed to several hundred subjects by the senior author at six national cross-gender club-sponsored events. One year later a total of 692 subjects had responded. The rate of return from all materials distributed was approximately 35%.

Demographic and Identifying Data

Age: Mean age was 43 years (range 17-77).

Marital status: Twenty-three percent had never married. Among the 77% who did marry, 52% had divorced. Of those divorced, 40% remarried. Forty-three percent reported living with their wife at this time. Concerning the wives, our subjects said 84% of them knew of the cross-gender activities of the husband. Of the informed wives, 38% were told prior to marriage and all except 13% learned about their husband's cross-genderism within the first five years of marriage.

Educational background: High school graduate = 92%. No college degree = 39%; A.A. degree = 10%; B.A. degree = 27%; M.A. degree = 17%; Doctoral degree = 7%.

Ethnicity: Caucasian = 92%. Black, Hispanic, Asian, and other racial origin were about 2% each.

Employment status: Working full-time = 78%; part-time = 7%; retired = 9%; unemployed 6%.

Geographic distribution: All parts of the United States were represented with most living on the eastern seaboard, the midwest, and the west coast. Three percent were from Canada, England, New Zealand and Australia.

Parenthood: Sixty percent reported having fathered at least one child.

Military service: Twenty-two percent reported some military service.

Hormones: Twenty-three percent said they were taking female hormones regularly.

Club affiliation: All except 21% reported membership in at least one support organization.

Self-Described Cross-Gender Status

Our participants were asked to describe the extent and periodicity of their cross-gender behavior using an 11 point descriptive scale. This self-description was used to classify our subjects into the following three groups; this is the basis for group classification used as the criterion in our validation procedure described below.

Transvestites. The category was comprised of episodic heterosexual cross dressers; most periodically appeared in public; considerable variation in frequency of cross dressing was reported. None lived full-time as women. N = 518 (76% of the entire sample).

Marginal Transvestites. These men were typically heterosexual episodic cross dressers who defined themselves as "a transsexual" although none were living full-time as women. N = 78 (11% of the entire sample).

Transsexuals. This category was comprised of biological males living full-time as women either with or without sexual reassignment. The critical determinant was that they occupied the cross-gender role continuously. We are quite certain this sample includes both so-called primary and secondary transsexuals with about 75% best described as secondary transsexuals. N = 86 (13%). Ten subjects did not provide the requested self-description data and were therefore excluded from the validation analysis.

Characteristics of This Subject Sample

The present subjects are a nonclinical sample with respect to how we obtained their cooperation. However, some are undoubtedly participating in individual or group counseling and some are participating in gender programs offering assessment of suitability for sex reassignment. A high percentage are affiliated with at least one cross-gender support group. Compared to subjects described by major gender identity clinics, this group is believed to be at least 10 years older, on the average, and probably less conflicted about their gender status than sex reassignment applicants. In general, this is a well educated group and most are employed full-time.

Validation and Cross-Validation Samples

Our sample of 692 subjects was divided randomly into two groups, each with 346 subjects. Exploratory factor analyses and initial development was carried out using the validation sample. Replication factor analysis and related item selection procedures were carried out with the cross-validation sample.

Item Preparation and Selection

The first version of the Cross-Gender Questionnaire consisted of 113 items designed to assess several levels of cross-gender behavior ranging from fantasies and plans for action through actual overt cross-gender behavior. It was developed, in part, from an earlier questionnaire which we had used to study a transvestite sample (Docter, 1988). Prior to writing items, the domain of constructs most prominent in describing cross-gender behavior was reviewed. These included, for example, sexual arousal, gender identity, periodic vs. sustained cross-gender behavior, role behavior in the cross-gender mode, sexual orientation, desire for sex reassignment, strength of masculine identity, and commitment to feminize the body. Items were written by the senior author based on these dimensions and upon his clinical experience with men manifesting variations in cross-gender fantasy and behavior. Pilot versions of the questionnaire were completed by twenty males who were self-described transvestites or transsexuals. The subjects were also invited to suggest additional items and editorial corrections. All items were to be answered, yes or no. The resulting 113 item version was completed by all subjects. Following the exploratory factor analysis and item selection procedures, the total number of items was reduced to 56. One additional item was eliminated through the replication factor analysis yielding a final total of 55 items.

RESULTS

Factor Analysis and Item Analysis: Validation Sample

Exploratory Factor Analysis

Exploratory factor analysis was conducted for the validation sample (principal components with fourth-power promax transformation). The EXPLORE program (Fleming, 1991) was used to conduct the analyses. A screen plot (Cattell, 1966) suggested that four factors would account for the data. Items with low communalities (< .20), on any factor, or which were complex (second highest loading > .35) were eliminated. A final analysis of the remaining 56 items was retained and interpreted. This analysis yielded four factors with associated eigenvalues of 13.7 (tapping 24.5% of the variance prior to rotation), 5.1 (9.1%), 3.4 (6.1%) and 2.9 (5.2%). After rotation the unique[1] variance explained by each factor was: AROUSE (5.10 or 9.1%); FEMIN (4.65, or 8.3%); IDENT (4.04 or 7.2%); ROLE (4.25 or 7.6%).

Some summary measures from the EXPLORE program are helpful in evaluating the fit of the final solution. Measures of sampling adequacy (Kaiser, 1981) for each variable are indicative of the item's appropriateness for factor analysis. All items had MSAs >.90, which is considered excellent, with the overall MSA = .99. Kaiser's (1974) index of factor simplicity (a measure of the tendency of variables to load on a single factor) was computed for each variable. Values above .90 are calibrated as "marvelous"; values between .80 and .90 are considered "meritorious." For the present data the overall IFS measure was .89 and the median was .90.

Of the 56 items, all loaded at least .40 on one of the factors. The average (root-mean-square) of salient items on each factor scale was in the .50s (range = .51-.58), whereas the average for nonsalient loadings was .02 or less. Only 7 had secondary loadings greater than .20 in absolute value, which included one with a loading over .30. There were 146 loadings in the hyperplane (using a criterion of plus or minus .15), or 87% of 168 possible in the ideal case of perfect "cluster" structure.

Factor Scales and Interpretation

Scale totals were formed by simple summation of the items that saturated each of the four factors. The scales were labeled: Cross-gender Identity (IDENT), Cross-gender Feminization (FEMIN), Cross-gender Sexual Arousal (AROUSE), and Cross-gender Social/Sexual Role (ROLE). Factor interpretations are as follows:

Cross-gender Identity (IDENT = 14 items). We believe this scale is measuring cross-gender self percepts and cross-gender identifications. High scores are believed predictive of sustained commitment to engage in cross-gender behavior. Low scores are predictive of episodic gender-exchanging. Here are examples of items on this scale: "I can experience feelings of being female at practically any time no matter how I am dressed." "I can enjoy being a woman, but at other times I enjoy functioning like a man." "If I must put aside my feminine role for even a short time, it is very hard for me to do so."

Cross-gender Feminization (FEMIN = 13 items). High scores are predictive of high motivation to feminize the male body, to achieve legally recognized feminine gender status, and to live entirely in the cross-gender mode. The following items are drawn from this scale: "I have lived entirely (or almost entirely) as a woman for 30 (or more) consecutive days." "I have taken female hormones regularly for six months or longer." "I have received a small amount (or more) of cosmetic surgery to improve my feminine appearance."

Cross-gender Sexual Arousal (AROUSE = 16 items). High scores denote an association, past or present, between cross-gender behavior and erotic arousal. These items are representative of this scale: "Sometimes I get a sexual thrill when I see my feminine image in a mirror." "Buying and using beautiful makeup will often make me feel sexually excited." "Often I become sexually excited when reading about men who become women."

Cross-gender Social/Sexual Role (ROLE = 12 items). High scores are associated with sustained commitment to taking the cross-gender role in real-life situations and social and sexual interactions with men when in the cross-gender mode. High scores reflect substantial role enactment not simply plans or fantasies of possible future action. Some representative items are: "While in the feminine role, I have been escorted to a restaurant by a man as his date." "While in the feminine role, I have been passionately kissed on the lips by a man" "While in the feminine role, I have had a physical sexual encounter with a man that went beyond kissing." Items also loaded on this scale (inversely) are those which indicated a predominant heterosexual orientation. For example: "As a man, I am exclusively attracted to women."

Reliabilities

Item-total correlations were formed using corrected total scores (i.e., scores with the score for the item being analyzed removed from the total), and KR-20 internal consistency reliabilities were computed for each of the four scales. The individual coefficients were: IDENT = .88; FEMIN = .92; AROUSE = .88; and ROLE = .86. Each of these was considered acceptable.

Factor Intercorrelations

As shown in Table 1, moderate intercorrelations were found among the four factors except for ROLE vs. AROUSE which did not correlate. This contrasts with frequent clinical reports which have held that more extreme cross-gender role-taking, as in trans-sexualism, was inversely related to cross-gender sexual arousal. The moderate relationships shown in Table 1 are consistent with clinical expectations.

Factor Analysis: Cross-Validation Sample

Replication of Exploratory Factor Analysis

An additional exploratory factor analysis was carried out using the 346 subjects in our cross-validation sample.[2] Four factors were again rotated as described above and 55 of the 56 items loaded as expected on their respective scales. However, six of the items met a selection criterion of only .35 rather than the .40 level employed in the validation analysis. One item which loaded only .30 was elimi-

Table 1

Correlations Among Four Factors

	IDENT	FEMIN	AROUSE	ROLE
IDENT	1.000			
FEMIN	.505*	1.000		
AROUSE	-.341*	-.426*	1.000	
ROLE	.366	.399*	-.013	1.00

* $p < .001$

nated from the questionnaire because of this low loading. Hence, the final number of items for the Cross-Gender Questionnaire was 55. The average loadings were again computed: for salients the averages ranged from .52 to .58 and for nonsalients all were .02 or less.

The three goodness-of-fit measures tested earlier were repeated for the cross-validation data with nearly identical results: overall measure of sampling adequacy (MSA) = .99; overall index of factor simplicity (IFS) = .90; percent nonsalients in hyperplane = 86%.

KR-20 reliabilities for the four factors identified in the replication analysis are also very similar to those reported for the validation sample: IDENT = .86; FEMIN = .92; AROUSE = .90; ROLE = .86.

Scale Differences Across Three Groups

As noted above, the respondents described their cross-gender status along a 12-point scale indicative of intensity of cross-genderism. Based on these responses three categories were defined: Transvestites (N = 518, 76%); Marginal transvestites (N = 78, 11%); and Transsexuals (N = 86, 13%). Ten subjects were not classifiable. A multivariate analysis of variance was conducted to examine differences in level of responding between these groups on the four factor scales. It was hypothesized that for each of the three scales other than Cross-gender Sexual Arousal the transvestite group would reveal the lowest factor mean scores and that the transsexuals would have the highest of the group means. Conversely, for the Sexual Arousal factor we predicted that the transvestites would show the highest mean with the transsexuals having the lowest. For all variables we predicted that the intermediate group of marginal transvestites would also have mean scores on all variables between the other two groups.

The means and standard deviations for the three groups on the scale scores are shown in Table 2, from which it is seen that the direction of differences are consistent with our predictions for each of the four variables. The results for the multivariate analysis were: $F(4,676) = 277.84, p \le .001$.

For the separate univariate tests the results were as follows: for IDENT, $F(1,679) = 271.75$; FEMIN, $F(1,679) = 961.44$; ROLE, $F(1,679) = 103.02$; AROUSE, $F(1,679) = 174.99$; with all $p \le .001$.

Step-down F-tests were also computed in which the variables were pre-ordered in terms of theoretical importance (Tabachnick & Fidell, 1988). The ordering was as listed in the above paragraph. Although this ordering is admittedly somewhat arbitrary, it does permit some control over Type I error.

The step-down tests were also conducted as one degree of freedom tests to test for monotonic trend ("linear" component). Such a pre-planned contrast permitted a more formalized testing of the hypotheses concerning the differences between the groups.

For the ordered tests the results of the test for linear component were: IDENT, $F(1,679) = 271.75 \, p \le .001$; FEMIN, $F(1,678) = 568.62, p \le .001$; ROLE, $F(1,677) = 10.43$, n.s.; and AROUSE, $F(1,676) = 15.14, p \le .001$.

From these results we see that, when taken separately, all scales are significantly different than chance. Controlling for the fact that

Table 2

Means and Standard Deviations for Four Factors Across Three Groups

Factor	Transvestites		Marginal Transvestites		Transsexuals	
	Mean	SD	Mean	SD	Mean	SD
IDENT	6.62	3.7	12.24	1.7	11.72	1.7
FEMIN	1.50	2.2	5.31	3.5	10.29	3.0
AROUSE	6.57	4.4	10.92	4.0	12.35	3.7
ROLE	3.68	3.4	5.59	3.5	7.38	3.0

scales are intercorrelated by ordering, however, the ROLE scale is not significant in the context of the step-down analysis.

DISCUSSION

Several investigators (for example, Blanchard, 1985b; Freund, Watson, & Dickey, 1991) have shown that self-report questionnaires are a potentially useful technique for differentiating among a heterogeneous group of transvestites and transsexuals. The questionnaire we have developed differs from all earlier reports in that ours includes a broader range of content and more questions for each scale than used in earlier measures. In theory, this would be expected to enhance reliability and validity.

A second important difference contrasting our study with earlier reports is that our subjects were not acquired through a clinical channel. We consider this important because clinicians have reported that many applicants for hormonal or genital sex reassignment tend to exaggerate their cross-gender histories somewhat to conform to what they believe the clinician wants to hear (Blanchard, Clemmensen, & Steiner, 1985). While no self-report questionnaire can assure truthful responding, at the least, such procedures offer a standard format for posing questions and permit the objective scoring of responses.

Starting with a validation sample of 346 transvestites and transsexuals, we have used factor analysis to identify four independent factors derived from the 55-item Cross-Gender Questionnaire. The factors are: (a) Cross-gender Identity, (b) Cross-gender Feminization, (c) Cross-gender Sexual Arousal, and (d) Cross-gender Social/Sexual Role. We have also shown that three measures of goodness-of-fit support a four factor solution. Factor reliabilities were satisfactory. Using a cross-validation sample of 346 similar subjects (drawn randomly from our total sample of 692 biological males), we repeated the processes of item selection and factor identification. Virtually identical results were found. The replicated factor analysis yielded the same four factors comprised of the same items with only a single item being eliminated due to a low factor loading.

Partial validation of the Cross-Gender Questionnaire is provided by analysis of variance results. Taken individually, each of our four factors yield mean scores which are significantly different for three groups: transvestites, marginal transvestites (borderline transsexuals), and transsexuals.

We believe these measures may supplement clinical interviewing by allowing an individual's scores to be compared to the norms for known groups. But beyond such possible assistance with differential assessment, an important advantage of using an objectively scorable questionnaire is that changes in scores for a given person can be followed over time. In some individuals, the cognitive and behavioral expressions of cross-gender behavior change considerably with experience; these measures are believed to offer promising tools for the measurement of such changes.

There may be typological implications of using measurements such as ours to better understand the variations within the syndromes of transvestism and transsexualism. For example, there is substantial clinical evidence that transvestism and transsexualism are global categories or syndromes of several related but different sub-types (for a review of typological issues see Docter, 1988). For example, the phenomena of primary and secondary transsexualism have been extensively described. With reference to various forms of transvestism, perhaps the best known division is into two major groups: so-called fetishistic transvestites and marginal transvestites. The clarification of typological questions is likely to depend upon the development of more refined assessment procedures.

In recent reports (Blanchard, 1991, 1992), the distinction is drawn between heterosexual males who express very persistent and intrusive fantasies of cross-gender ideation but do not cross dress, and their counterparts who do cross dress. Blanchard presents a compelling case for taking a new view of transvestism so as to accommodate men who, at a cognitive level, seem to love themselves as women yet do not act upon these fantasy scripts with overt cross-gender conduct. Blanchard advocates the term *autogynephelia* (love of oneself as a woman) to describe the entire spectrum of such self-love, from fantasy alone, through cross-dressing and social role taking as a woman in both transvestites and transsexuals. Blanchard (1992) provides data to support his claim that all gender dysphoric heterosexual males not sexually aroused by other males are aroused by the thought or image of themselves as women. As Blanchard notes and as we stress in our earlier publication (Docter, 1988), it is the cognitive representations and the reinforcing value of these thought patterns which may be of great importance in understanding the etiology of many expressions of cross-gender behavior. This generalization applies across the entire complex and multi-dimensional matrix of the many cross-gender behavior patterns. No existing questionnaire samples all of what will need to be measured to tap both the fantasy processes and the lifestyles of males expressing cross-gender behavior, but Blanchard's theoretical approach and what we offer here may be steps in the right direction.

Finally, we urge that these measures and others like them be used to supplant the ill-defined construct of gender dysphoria. In our view, this term does not appear to have any psychometrically acceptable operational definition. Gender dysphoria is a construct which is currently expected to explain and describe more than it was invented for. It is often applied to cross-gender phenomena having nothing to do with any sort of dysphoria. We propose that the scales of cross-genderism described here, together with other measurement procedures, offer more accurate ways to communicate about the variables of importance in transvestism and transsexualism than does the vague construct of gender dysphoria. What is most needed to advance understanding of cross-gender phenomena is an insistence that major constructs be operationally defined, that theoretical formulations be linked to the mainstream of psychological theory, and that simplistic and incomplete diagnostic formulations be put aside until the framework for a data-based typology is formulated.

NOTES

1. In oblique analysis the proportion of explained variance cannot be partitioned exactly among the factors because of their intercorrelations. The unique variance is a measure of the non-overlapping variance accounted for by each factor.

2. Confirmatory factor analysis methods provide more powerful tests of structural hypotheses concerning the number and the nature of hypothesized factors (e.g., Joreskog & Sorbom, 1989). Such methods could not be used with the present data, however, for two reasons: (a) there were a very large number of items relative to the number of subjects, and (b) the most widely used methods require normally distributed variables, an assumption that could not be met with these dichotomous items.

REFERENCES

Althof, S. E., Lothstein, L. M., Jones, P. & Shen, J. (1983). An MMPI subscale (Gd) to identify males with gender identity conflicts. *Journal of Personality Assessment, 47,* 42-49.

Blanchard, R. (1985a). Typology of male-to-female transsexualism. *Archives of Sexual Behavior, 14,* 247-261.

Blanchard, R. (1985b). Research methods for the typological study of gender disorders in males. In B. W. Steiner (Ed.), *Gender dysphoria* (pp. 227-257). New York: Plenum Press.

Blanchard, R. (1989a). The concept of autogynephilia and the typology of male gender dysphoria. *Journal of Nervous and Mental Disease, 177,* 616-623.

Blanchard, R. (1989b). The classification and labeling of nonhomosexual gender dysphorics. *Archives of Sexual Behavior, 18,* 315-334.

Blanchard, R. (1991). Clinical observations and systematic studies of autogynephilia. *Journal of Sex & Marital Therapy, 17,* 235-251.

Blanchard, R. (1992). Nonmonotonic relation of autogynephilia and heterosexual attraction. *Journal of Abnormal Psychology, 101,* 271-276.

Blanchard, R., Clemmensen, L. H., & Steiner, B. W. (1985). Social desirability response set and systematic distortion in the self-report of adult male gender patients. *Archives of Sexual Behavior, 14,* 505-516.

Cattell, R. B. (1966). The screen test for the number of factors. *Multivariate Behavioral Research, 1,* 245-276.

Docter, R. F. (1988). *Transvestites and transsexuals: Toward a theory of cross-gender behavior.* New York: Plenum Press.

Fleming, J. S. (1991). *EXPLORE: A program for exploratory common factor analysis and related models* (Computer program). Northridge, CA: Author.

Freund, K. (1985). Cross-gender identity in a broader context. In B. W. Steiner (Ed.), *Gender dysphoria* (pp. 259-324). New York: Plenum Press.

Freund, K., Langevin, R., Satterberg, J., & Steiner, B. (1977). Extension of the gender identity scale for males. *Archives of Sexual Behavior, 6,* 507-519.

Freund, K., Nagler, E., Langevin, R., Zajac, A., & Steiner, B. W. (1974). Measuring feminine gender identity in homosexual males. *Archives of Sexual Behavior, 3,* 249-260.

Freund, K., Steiner, B. W., & Chan, S. (1982). Two types of cross gender identity. *Archives of Sexual Behavior, 11,* 49-63.

Freund, K., Watson, R., & Dickey, R. (1991). The types of heterosexual gender identity disorder. *Annals of Sex Research, 4,* 93-105.

Joreskog, K. G., & Sorbom, D. (1988). *LISREL VII. Analysis of linear relationships by maximum likelihood, instrumental variables, and least squares methods.* Mooresville, IN.: Scientific Software, Inc.

Kaiser, H. F. (1974). An index of factor simplicity. *Psychometrika, 39,* 31-35.

Kaiser, H. F. (1981). A revised measure of sampling adequacy for factor-analytic data matrices. *Educational and Psychological Measurement, 41,* 379-381.

Langevin, R., Majpruz, V., & Handy, L. (1990). The gender dysphoria scale: A comparison of gender patients, sexually anomalous patients, and community controls. *Annals of Sex Research, 2,* 91-96.

Renaissance Education Association, Inc. (1991). *Renaissance News.* P.O. Box 1263, King of Prussia, PA 19406-0552.

Tabachnick, B. G., & Fidell, L. S. (1988). *Using multivariate statistics* (2nd ed.). New York: Harper & Row.

APPENDIX

The Cross-Gender Questionnaire

(Experimental version 2.0)

Richard F. Docter, Ph.D. and James S. Fleming, Ph.D.
California State University, Northridge

Please respond to each item by showing whether it is MORE TRUE or MORE FALSE. Please mark in the TRUE (T) or FALSE (F) box. Please respond to all items.

T F

[ ] [ ] 1. When I wear womens' clothing I do not consider it "cross dressing" because my true gender is feminine (or mostly feminine).

[ ] [ ] 2. I have an alternative "fantasy cross dressing wardrobe" which is too sexy to wear in public.

[ ] [ ] 3. I have adopted a feminine name which is now my legal name.

[ ] [ ] 4. If I am wearing a sexy dress I sometimes feel more attracted to men.

[ ] [ ] 5. I believe I am a "woman in a man's body."

6. Sometimes I have acquired more sets of fancy underwear or other sexy clothing than I need.

[ ] [ ]

7. I have a driver's license or other valid identification showing my "female" picture and name.

[ ] [ ]

8. I eat in restaurants in my feminine role several times a year.

[ ] [ ]

9. In my feminine role, I usually feel like I am a woman.

[ ] [ ]

10. Sometimes I get a sexual thrill when I see my feminine image in a mirror.

[ ] [ ]

11. While in the feminine role, men I did not know have bought me refreshments or drinks.

[ ] [ ]

12. I have lived entirely (or almost entirely) as a woman for more than six consecutive months.

[ ] [ ]

13. I prefer to think of my feminine name as my real name.

[ ] [ ]

[ ] [ ] 14. While in the feminine role, I have been escorted to a restaurant by a man as his date.

[ ] [ ] 15. When I feel tense, wearing something feminine will usually make me feel a little more calm.

[ ] [ ] 16. I have lived entirely (or almost entirely) as a woman for one year or longer.

[ ] [ ] 17. I can experience feelings of being female at any time no matter how I am dressed.

[ ] [ ] 18. Buying and using beautiful makeup will often make me feel sexually excited.

[ ] [ ] 19. I have received 10 or more hours of electrolysis.

[ ] [ ] 20. I have received 50 or more hours of electrolysis.

[ ] [ ] 21. While in the feminine role, I have been escorted to some kind of entertainment event by a man on a date.

[ ] [ ] 22. Even when not in the feminine role I reveal some feminine mannerisms (or I used to).

[ ] [ ] 23. Putting on lipstick or perfume often makes me feel erotic or sexy.

[ ] [ ] 24. I can enjoy being a woman, but at other times I enjoy functioning like a man.

[ ] [ ] 25. I often prefer sexy hosiery and high heels to the more ordinary style many women wear.

[ ] [ ] 26. Being in the feminine role is almost always a sexually arousing experience for me.

[ ] [ ] 27. While in the feminine role, I have danced with a man.

[ ] [ ] 28. Wearing beautiful lingerie usually gives me some sexual excitement.

29. When in my feminine role I feel I am expressing my "true self," not putting on an act.

[ ] [ ]

30. I have talked to a physician about obtaining female hormones (whether you did obtain them or not).

[ ] [ ]

31. While in the feminine role, I have been passionately kissed on the lips by a man.

[ ] [ ]

32. If it were possible, I'd choose to live my life as a woman (or I now do so).

[ ] [ ]

33. Some specific articles of clothing usually have an especially powerful effect on my sexual arousal.

[ ] [ ]

34. I have taken female hormones regularly for three months or longer.

[ ] [ ]

35. While in the feminine role, I have had a physical encounter with a man that went beyond kissing.

[ ] [ ]

36. If I must put aside my feminine role for even a short time, it is very hard for me to do so.

[ ] [ ]

37. Wearing beautiful clothes and makeup often brings me greater sexual pleasure than other sexual activities.

[ ] [ ]

38. Often I become sexually excited just thinking about being a woman.

[ ] [ ]

39. I have taken female hormones regularly for six months or longer.   [ ] [ ]

40. As a man, I am exclusively attracted to women.   [ ] [ ]

41. I almost always wear one or more items of feminine apparel under my male clothes.   [ ] [ ]

42. I often become sexually excited when I shop for womens' clothing, shoes, or makeup.   [ ] [ ]

43. I have taken female hormones regularly for one year or longer.   [ ] [ ]

44. As a man, I am attracted to both women and men (not necessarily equally).   [ ] [ ]

45. I daydream or think about being a woman at least once a day.   [ ] [ ]

46. Often I become sexually excited when I read about men who become women.   [ ] [ ]

47. I have discussed with a physician possible (or actual) cosmetic surgery to improve my feminine appearance.   [ ] [ ]

48. In the feminine role, I am exclusively attracted to women.   [ ] [ ]

49. I daydream or think about being a woman at least 10 times each day.   [ ] [ ]

50. Being in the feminine role is a super-pleasure for me.   [ ] [ ]

51. I have received a small amount (or more) of cosmetic surgery to improve my feminine appearance.   [ ] [ ]

52. When in the feminine role, I am attracted to both men and women (Not necessarily equally).   [ ] [ ]

[ ] [ ]   53. After several hours (or days) in the feminine role I'm usually ready to change back into mens' clothes.

[ ] [ ]   54. Being in the feminine role often produces strong feelings of exhilaration.

[ ] [ ]   55. On one (or more) occasions, while in the feminine role I have had a sexual encounter with a man.

==

Scoring procedure: Obtain a total score for each scale by adding the items answered *yes* and the items answered *no.*

IDENT: Cross-Gender Identity *yes* items: 1, 5, 9, 13, 17, 22, 29, 32, 36, 41, 45, 49

No items: 24, 53.

FEMIN: Cross Gender Feminization *yes* items: 3, 7, 8, 12, 16, 19, 20, 30, 34, 39, 43, 47, 51.

Hormone Treatment in Transsexuals

Henk Asscheman, MD
Louis J.G. Gooren, MD

INTRODUCTION

Except for the sex chromosomes and gonads all bodily differences between men and women must be attributed to the actions of sex hormones. While the inherent tendency of the prenatal human organism is to develop along female lines, prenatal differentiation as a male depends on testicular hormones (Mullerian–inhibiting–hormone and testosterone and its derivates). The wider bony pelvis in girls in comparison with boys, is probably dependent on local effects of prenatal ovarian estrogen production. There is no known fundamental difference in sensitivity to the biological action of sex steroids on the basis of the genetic patterns of 46,XY and 46,XX.

The prepubertal period is hormonally relatively quiescent (Conte, Grumbach, Kaplan & Reiter, 1980). The hormones of puberty accentuate sex differences. Testosterone and its potent derivate 5alpha-dihydrotestosterone (DHT) induce penile growth and secondary sex characteristics as sexual hair, deepening of the voice, a muscular build and the greater average height in males in comparison to the females. In girls, estrogens in conjunction with progestagens induce breast formation and a fat distribution predominantly around the hips; subcutaneous fat padding produces a softness of the body configuration and of the skin. The skin in women is further generally less oily than in men; the latter on the basis of activation of the sebaceous glands by androgens.

Henk Asscheman and Louis J.G. Gooren are both affiliated with the Division of Andrology/Endocrinology, Free University Hospital, Amsterdam.

Please send all correspondence to: Professor Louis J.G. Gooren, Free University Hospital, P.O. Box 7057, 1007 MB Amsterdam, the Netherlands.

Fundamental to sex reassignment treatment is the acquisition to the fullest extent possible of the sex characteristics of the other sex. With the exception of the internal and external genitalia, these characteristics are contingent of the biological effects of the respective sex steroids. Therefore (semi)synthetic sex steroids are indispensable tools in sex reassignment treatment. The use of cross-gender hormone treatment is associated with a better outcome (Hamburger, 1969; Leavitt et al., 1980).

The "two year real-life test" (Money & Ambinder, 1978) is pivotal in diagnostic-therapeutic approach of gender dysphoria. It allows both the gender-dysphoric subject and the psychologist/physician to examine whether sex reassignment relieves the burden of gender dysphoria. The emerging physical changes associated with cross-gender sex hormone treatment will facilitate the assumption of the role as a member of the other sex both in private life and in society.

The attempt to induce cross-gender sex characteristics in transsexuals–generally biologically normally differentiated males and females in their adult years–can be subdivided into two aspects:

1. Annihilation of sex characteristics of the original sex.
2. Induction of sex characteristics of the sex one reckons oneself to belong to.

1. Unfortunately, the annihilation of sex characteristics of the original sex is incomplete. In male-to-female transsexuals, there is no mode of treatment to revert earlier effects of androgens on the skeleton. The greater height, the shape of the jaws, the size and shape of the hands and feet, and the narrow width of the pelvis can not be redressed once they have reached their final size at the end of puberty. Conversely, the relative lower height in female-to-male transsexuals (in the Netherlands an average of 12 cms) and the broader hip configuration will not change under the influence of hormonal treatment.

2. While in the majority of female-to-male transsexuals, a complete and inconspicuously masculine development can be induced with androgenic hormones, the effects of feminizing hormone treatment in male-to-female transsexuals can be objectively unsatisfactory with regard to reduction of male-type of facial/beard hair and induction of breast development.

Transsexuals often expect and sometimes demand rapid and complete changes immediately after the start of the hormonal therapy. The induced effects of cross-sex hormones are, however, limited and appear only gradually. Before starting hormone treatment a clear discussion of the possible changes and the limits in an individual patient, is indispensable in order to prevent unrealistic expectations. In the next and following sections we describe the effects of cross-gender hormones separately for male-to-female and female-to-male transsexual subjects.

Which Hormones and Which Dose?

For each of the above mentioned aspects of hormone treatment exists a large array of (semi) synthetic sex steroids. There are no solid literature data to prove certain hormonal drugs superior in efficacy to others. Only two published studies give an indication of the value of different hormone schedules in the treatment of transsexuals, but the results are far from conclusive (Meyer et al., 1981 & 1986). The choice of hormonal drugs in the treatment of transsexualism depends on availability (national regulations, pharmaceutical marketing), local traditions, side effects, route of administration, cost and folk belief (in particular from the side of the transsexual subject and his/her peer group, but also from the physician). Optimal dosages of these drugs have not yet been established.

The first effects of the cross-gender sex hormones appear already after 6 to 8 weeks (Futterweit, 1980). Voice changes in female-to-male transsexuals and the development of painful breast noduli in male-to-female transsexuals are the first manifestations. Thereafter the changes take over 6 to 24 months and even longer before they are complete (beard growth may take 4 to 5 years in androgen-treated female-to-male transsexuals).

Cross-Sex Hormone Treatment in Male-to-Female Transsexuals

Annihilation of Male Characteristics

In male-to-female transsexuals suppression of the original sex characteristics can be obtained by compounds that exert directly or indirectly an antiandrogenic effect. Androgens are for their production dependent on stimulation by the pituitary hormone luteinizing hormone (LH) which, in turn, is stimulated by the hypothalamic hormone luteinizing hormone-releasing hormone (LHRH). The biological action of androgens is contingent on their interaction with hormone receptors in the body's tissue cells. Interference with any of these mechanisms will lead to a decline of the biological action of androgenic hormone. Some of the drugs that will be listed have a dual action in this respect (Table 1).

1. Suppression of gonadotropins (the pituitary hormones) that stimulate testicular and ovarian hormone production can be achieved by LHRH analogues: triptorelin and leuprorelin 3.75 mg/4 weeks are available as injectables. Their cost is prohibitive; a major side effect is hot flashes of the type that postmenopausal women experience. There is no reported experience with these drugs in transsexuals. Also cyproterone acetate, progestagens and high dose estrogens suppress gonadotropins by their negative feedback action. Progestagens are available in the form of medroxyprogesterone acetate (Provera^R) as a parenteral drug (150 mg/6 weeks) or oral drug (5-10 mg/day). They probably also interfere with the androgen receptor.

2. Interference with the production of testosterone or its conversion to the potent metabolite 5alpha-dihydrotestosterone (DHT) can be exercised by drugs like spironolactone (Aldactone^R) 100-200 mg/day. Finasteride is a potent 5 alpha-reductase inhibitor preventing the conversion of testosterone to DHT and therewith reducing its biological effect.

3. Drugs that interfere with receptor binding of androgens (or in the future with postreceptor mechanisms) have been used successfully. Cyproterone acetate (Androcur^R) 100 mg/day orally or 300 mg/month intramuscularly and less effectively medroxyprogesterone acetate have also antigonadotropic action. The "pure" antiandrogens nilutamide (Anandron^R) 300 mg/day and flutamide (Eulexin 250 mg, three times a day) are potent drugs. They are less suited as monotherapy since by their interference with the negative feedback action of androgens, they stimulate gonadotropin production and subsequently androgen production. Spironolactone has also receptor-blocking properties.

TABLE 1. Hormones Used in Cross-Gender Hormone Treatment of Transsexualism

Antiandrogens

LHRH analogues:

leuprorelin	Lucrin depot[R]	3.75 mg/months s.c.
triptorelin	Decapeptyl-CR[R]	3.75 mg/months i.m.

Interference with testosterone or DHT production:

spironolactone	Aldactone[R]	100–200 mg/day p.o.
finasteride	not registered	
flutamide	Eulexin[R]	250 mg t.i.d., p.o.

Antigonadotropic:

cyproterone acetate	Androcur[R]	100–150 mg/day p.o.
	Provera[R]	5–10 mg/day p.o.
medroxyprogesterone	Depo-Provera[R]	150 mg/month i.m.
	Farlutal[R]	5–10 mg/day p.o.
	Farlutal depot	100 mg/month i.m.

Androgenreceptor blockers:

cyproterone acetate	Androcur[R]	100–150 mg/day p.o.
nilutamide	Anandron[R]	300 mg/day p.o.
spironolactone	Aldactone[R]	100–200 mg/day p.o.

Estrogens:

ethinyl estradiol	Lynoral[R]	100 µg/day p.o.
conjugated estrogens	Premarin[R]	5–10 mg/day p.o.
17β estradiol	Progynova[R]	2–4 mg/day p.o.
	Progynon depot[R]	10 mg/2 weeks to 100 mg/month i.m.
	Estraderm TTS[R]	50–100 µg/day transdermally
estriol	Synapause[R]	4–6 mg/day p.o.

Androgens:

testosterone esters	Testoviron[R]	250 mg/2 weeks i.m.
	Sustanon[R]	250 mg/2 weeks i.m.
testosterone undecanoate	Andriol[R]	160–240 mg/day p.o.

Of all the above drugs side-effects have been reported. Some are inherent in the interference with the biological action of androgens like a reduction of muscle mass and power and of the hemoglobin content. Some patients will complain of loss of energy and vitality to straightforward depression. The antiandrogen we have extensively used is cyproterone acetate (100mg/day). Side effects encountered are those mentioned above. Our alternative drug is spironolactone. Several studies have demonstrated its efficacy in transsexuals and in hirsute women alike. It has also an antihypertensive effect, since the drug was designed as a diuretic.

We have limited experience with nilutamide and LHRH antagonists. Medroxy-progesterone acetate has been widely used in the USA also in sex offenders. It is a satisfactory drug also in the view of the mild side effects and the costs. A randomized double-blind clinical trial to establish the best suited antiandrogen compound in transsexuals has not been performed so far.

Following orchiectomy we try to reduce or terminate antiandrogen therapy. Sexual hair growth is clearly dependent on androgens for its initiation and it would be logical to believe that antiandrogens are redundant following orchiectomy. Though not verified by research data, patients claim that also after orchiectomy their sexual hair growth is still reduced by antiandrogens. Due to the much shorter life cycle of sexual hair on the trunk, arms and legs as compared to the face and the greater density of hair follicles in the beard area, beard growth is not reduced to a cosmetically acceptable degree by antiandrogens. Other measures like depilation by electrolysis are needed. Those subjects who are young enough to have no significant beard development or whose racial background provides them with little or no beard development, are not in need of antiandrogens for this purpose.

Induction of Female Characteristics

The principal feminizing hormones are estrogens. Estrogens alone can induce most typical female characteristics as has been shown in cases of Turner syndrome in which the ovaries fail to produce hormones. A second sex steroid produced by the ovaries is progesterone. It prime function is to prepare the uterine mucosa for nidation. Its feminizing effect is probably limited, but effects of breast tissue have been described. Meyer et al. (1986) found no difference in breast hemicircumference between male-to-female transsexuals who had used estrogens only and those who had used both estrogens and progestagens, but this study was not a randomized double-blind clinical investigation.

It has been suggested that "unopposed action of estrogens" (by progestagens) would constitute a risk factor for carcinomas of the breast and there are epidemiological data in support of this. On the other hand studies in users of oral contraceptives have suggested that progestagens play a role in breast cancer development, though oral contraceptives overall are associated with a reduced risk of breast cancer. Three cases of breast carcinomas in male-to-female transsexuals have been published but it is difficult to arrive at statistically reliable conclusions on risks since the total number of users is unknown and no data are available on what estrogens and how long these three subjects have been taking this medication. Of note is the fact that breast carcinomas have not been observed in men with prostatic carcinoma taking high doses of estrogens but the follow-up may have been too short in view of their lethal disease. Male-to-female transsexuals should be informed about this risk factor. As with the general female population, they should receive information on self-examination of their breasts. At medical check-ups their breasts should be physically examined and if palpation is suspect, mammography and eventually biopsy should follow. The fact that transsexuals have often breast implants may impede physical (self)examination of the breast. In our population of more than 500 hormonally treated male-to-female transsexuals (follow-up 0-20 years with an estimated median of 6.5 years) we have not come across a case of breast carcinoma.

In terms of estrogenic effects there is no superior estrogen. The choice depends mainly on availability, costs and the preference of the subject. Careful clinical studies on side effects in the form of randomized double-blind placebo-controlled studies with different estrogens are non-existent. The chemical formula and the route of administration lead to substantial differences in characteristics of estrogenic drugs. All oral estrogens first pass the liver after intestinal absorption and exert an effect on liver metabolism, evidenced by their effects on lipids, clotting factors and renin. The liver metabolism of estrogen is also related to the chemical formula of the estrogen. Ethinyl estradiol is slowly metabolized whereas 17beta-estradiol is broken down rather rapidly, explaining the 10-20 fold difference in daily dosage. Concomitant drug use (anti-epileptics) may induce a more rapid metabolism of estrogens.

1. Ethinyl estradiol (Lynoral[R]), 50 µg orally twice (or more) daily, is the most potent estrogenic drug. It is a chemical modification of 17ß-estradiol, the main estrogen of the body, and it is slowly metabolized by the liver, but has a large effect on other metabolic pathways in the liver. It is very cheap, easily available worldwide and often used by male-to-female transsexuals because it can be obtained from women friends or without prescription in many countries as the oral contraceptive pill (always combined with progestagens). In the current estradiol assays its presence is not measured but the resulting suppression of gonadotropins suggests its use. A specific assay for ethinyl estradiol is commercially available.

2. "Natural" estrogens, which are not natural but metabolized estrogens from other species (pregnant mare urine) are more appropriately called conjugated estrogens (Premarin[R] and other brands). Active dose in postmenopausal women is 0.625-1.25 mg, but for cross-gender hormone therapy the active dose is 5-10 mg (Meyer et al., 1986). They are largely metabolized at first liver passage. It is said that they have less side effects than other estrogens. However, the supporting scientific evidence is very weak and in trials of secondary prevention of myocardial infarction in men, conjugated estrogens in a dose of 2.5 and 5 mg orally per day are clearly associated with an increased risk of thrombosis. Paradoxically, low doses appear to reduce the risk of cardiovascular disease in postmenopausal women.

3. 17ß-Estradiol (or in short estradiol) is the most potent of the three forms of native estrogens in the human body. It is produced synthetically and can be administered orally (Progynova[R], Estrofem[R], Zumenon[R] 2-4 mg per day) metabolized in great part at first liver passage, intramuscularly (Progynon-Depot[R] 20-200 mg per month) or transdermally (Estraderm TTS[R] 100 µg, patches are replaced twice weekly). In particular, this latter form is very promising because of its low number of estrogen-induced side effects.

However, its efficacy in cross-gender hormone treatment has not been fully determined (a study is in progress at our clinic). A considerable number of patients ($\pm 10\%$) have skin problems at the application site and its sticking qualities can be a problem in patients that perspire easily or in a hot climate. Another obstacle is the price (US\$ 1.00 per day), it is the most expensive estrogen therapy.

4. Estriol (Synapause E3[R], Ovestin[R] 2-6 mg orally per day) is a less potent native estrogen that is used in postmenopausal women for atrophic vaginitis and for urinary problems. In cross-gender hormone treatment high doses are necessary and estriol has no advantages over estradiol for this indication.

In our clinic ethinyl estradiol 100 µg orally per day has been the standard treatment for all male-to-female transsexuals until recently. With the introduction of transdermal estrogen we have changed our policy because of the frequent occurrence of thromboembolism in patients over 40 years of age (12%, Asscheman, Gooren & Eklund, 1989). All new male-to-female transsexuals older than 40 years are treated with Estraderm TTS[R] 100 µg two patches per week from the start. Younger patients are offered the same possibility but they are informed that their risk of thromboembolism is much lower (2.1%) and ethinyl estradiol 100 µg is proposed as an alternative. Intramuscular estrogen depots are not routinely given for two reasons. First, in case of side effects, not infrequent with estrogen therapy, it can take weeks before the serum levels of estradiol have normalized and second, male-to-female transsexuals tend to abuse estrogens under the wrong assumption "the more the better." We have seen subjects who used 800 mg Progynon-Depot[R], intramuscularly, per week with sometimes serious side effects (Gooren, Assies, Asscheman, de Slegte & van Kessel, 1988). With oral administration abuse is also not uncommon, but the doses are not so extreme.

After sex reassignment surgery we try to reduce the dose to a minimum that produces no clinical symptoms of sex hormone deficiency, but no lower than the minimum dose that protects against osteoporosis. In postoperative patients all kinds of estrogen substitution therapy are used depending on the personal preference of the transsexual patient and the lack of clinical symptoms of estrogen deficiency or side effects. Practically, this is similar to the estrogen treatment of postmenopausal women with some advantages: there is no need for progestagens and no risk of endometrial carcinoma.

Cross-Sex Hormone Treatment in Female-to-Male Transsexuals

Annihilation of Female Characteristics

The effects of estrogens on physical characteristics cannot be annihilated by antihormones. Antiestrogens administered to eugonadal women stimulate gonadotropin and subsequently ovarian hormone secretion. Theoretically, LHRH antagonists could be used. The objections have been mentioned earlier.

Transsexuals very much appreciate that their menstrual periods are terminated. This can be accomplished by progestagens with their antigonadotropic properties: medroxyprogesterone acetate (Provera[R], Farlutal[R]) 5 mg 1 à 2 tablets/day or 150 mg intramuscularly/3 months, lynesterol (Orgametril[R]) 5 mg or norethisterone (Primolut N[R]) 5 mg both 1 or 2 tablets/day. Androgens to be discussed in the next section have in high dosages also antigonadotropic action. There is no clear advantage in the combination of the two hormones unless androgens alone suppress menstrual bleeding insufficiently.

Induction of Male Characteristics

Androgens exert a powerful effect on the virilization process but completion may take as long as 2-4 years and sometimes even longer. The individual outcome depends on genetic factors both familial and racial. The degree of hairiness of siblings is a fair predictor of the virilization process.

To be used are testosterone esters 200-250 mg/2 weeks intramuscularly. Their brand names vary from place to place (Sustanon[R], Testoviron[R]). As oral androgens testosterone undecanoate can be mentioned (Andriol[R]) 160-240 mg/day, not available in the USA. With the latter preparation, menstrual bleeding is insufficiently suppressed in 50% of the patients and addition of a progestagen is required. The use of oral androgens with an alkyl group in the 17α position of the molecule is obsolete due to its hepatotoxicity. Oral androgens as mesterolone and fluoxymesterone are too weak for the induction of virilization.

In approximately 50-60% of the female-to-male transsexuals acne will occur. In 10-15% it is rather serious requiring dermatological treatment. It is now certain that androgen treatment has an unfavorable effect on the lipid profile. It places female-to-male transsexuals in the risk category of men. Therefore they must be advised not to smoke, to exercise moderately and to prevent overweight and high blood pressure.

Effects of Cross-Gender Hormones in Male-to-Female Transsexuals

Annihilation of the male pattern is possible for a number of secondary sex characteristics but only to a limited extent. Reduction of androgen-dependent hair growth with cyproterone acetate and ethinyl estradiol is fairly effective on the trunk and the limbs, but has a very limited success in the face. The body hair does not disappear but following suppression of androgen-dependent growth, the hair becomes less coarse and less visible, resembling the vellus hair on the female body in certain body regions. If hairlessness of the body is desired, only electrolysis is effective. Waxing and shaving can result in temporary hairlessness, which can be prolonged by the decrease in hair growth associated with estrogen and antiandrogen treatment. The beard hairs also become thinner and softer after several years of hormone use. Unfortunately, once the beard growth has fully developed and regular shaving is necessary, the result of antiandrogens alone is cosmetically unacceptable. Only electrolysis is effective in eliminating beard growth. In a few patients who had started treatment before developing visible hair growth, electrolysis could be avoided. After starting hormone treatment, male type scalp hair loss (masculine alopecia) ceases. Regrowth of scalp hair on bald areas is incomplete and of the vellus type. Hairstyle, hair implants or artificial hair techniques ("weaving," partial wigs) can successfully mask the masculine alopecia while hormones can at best make a minor contribution.

Penis length is not reduced by hormones, but due to its almost continuous flaccid state and an increase in lower abdominal fat, may appear reduced. Spontaneous erections are suppressed within 3 months but during erotic arousal erections still occur in the majority of our patients, evidencing the relative androgen-independence of this type of erection. Testicular volume is reduced by 25% within the first year of hormone use. This reduction is appreciated as a sign of progress and also makes hiding of the male genitals easier.

Induction of female characteristics is quite variable. In the initial phase of estrogen therapy, subareolar nodules which can be painful (Futterweit, 1980), are common. The breast size can be quantified by measuring the maximum hemicircumference over the nipple with a flexible ruler (either in the supine position or sitting which is our method). The increase in breast size evolves gradually with often periods of growth and periods of apparent standstill. The mean hemicircumference after 1 year is 10 cm in the supine position and 14 cm in the sitting position (the latter varies from 4 to 22 cm in our patients) and reaches its maximum after 18 to 24 months. In our patients the mean value is 18 cm, but it can vary from 4 to 28 cm. For comparison: in biological females it varies from 12 to 36 cm with a mean of 22 cm (own unpublished observations in a small number of these women). The values in male-to-female transsexuals are several centimeters less than in biological women. Moreover, the width of the male thorax is in general larger than that of the female thorax. Consequently, the proportional effect is judged as unsatisfactory by almost 50% of the male-to-female transsexual subjects. The majority of those unsatisfied requests surgical breast implants. In more than 50% of the male-to-female transsexuals, the estrogen-induced breast size is judged as satisfactory by the transsexual subject herself, obviating breast surgery. In a small number of subjects unilateral or bilateral subcutaneous mastectomy has been performed because of pubertal gynecomastia. The hormonal effect on operated breasts is nil. In the latter cases early breast implants are indicated, but we prefer to wait at least one year before recommending any surgery including breast surgery.

In male-to-female transsexuals, estrogens do not affect the pitch of the voice, and a low voice can be a great handicap. Speech therapy is necessary to achieve a more feminine vocal range. Vocal cord surgery does not obviate the need for speech therapy in almost all cases, but the resulting higher pitched voice facilitates a female public presentation.

The subcutaneous and intra-abdominal fat distribution is sex steroid-dependent. Males preferentially accumulate fat in the upper abdomen ("apples") and females around the hips ("pears"). Estrogen treatment results generally in more fat around the hips but this is not the rule and can vary largely. Skeletal structures like jaws, size of hands and form of the pelvis do not change with the estrogen and/or antiandrogen treatment.

Not infrequently male-to-female transsexuals complain of a dry skin and fragile nails. This is a consequence of the reduction in sebaceous gland activity following antiandrogen treatment. Avoidance of detergents and application of ointment is mostly helpful.

Effects of antiandrogens alone or in combination with estrogens on the mood and the emotional functioning are often reported by our patients and their partners. Definitive scientific proof in transsexuals that they are hormone-related is not available, but it is likely. In view of the consistency of these subjective reports and some studies in hypogonadal patients after substitution with appropriate hormones, an effect of hormones on the brain and consequently on brain functions like mood, is highly plausible.

Effects of Cross-Gender Hormones in Female-to-Male Transsexuals

Generally the virilization process proceeds subjectively and objectively in a satisfactory way and female-to-male transsexuals are pleased with it. It has no effect on their breast size. An oily skin and acne may become a problem. In comparison to other men they are rather short, but a short man is less conspicuous than a tall woman. The clitoris enlarges in all subjects though in a different degree. It sometimes suffices to have vaginal intercourse with a female partner, but that is not the rule. Most subjects indicate an increase of their libido following androgen treatment. Like male-to-female transsexuals female-to-male transsexuals must continue androgen treatment after ovariectomy to prevent hot flashes, loss of male characteristics and above all osteoporosis.

SIDE EFFECTS OF CROSS-GENDER HORMONE

Few systematic studies on side effects of cross-gender hormone treatment in transsexuals have been published. Meyer et al. (1986) found in 90 transsexuals only liver enzyme abnormalities and mild elevations of serum cholesterol and triglycerides. Case reports have described pulmonary embolism, cerebral thrombosis, myocardial infarction, prostatic metaplasia, and breast cancer in estrogen-treated male-to-female transsexuals and recurrent myocardial infarction in a female-to-male transsexual treated with androgens.

In 1989 we published a retrospective study on mortality and morbidity in 303 male-to-female and 122 female-to-male transsexuals who have been treated and followed at our clinic for 6 months to more than 13 years (Asscheman, Gooren & Eklund, 1989). Mortality in male-to-female transsexuals was 6-fold increased compared with the general population. This was in particular due to suicide and death by unknown cause. No deaths occurred in the female-to-male group but the median age was much lower. Side effects were common in the male-to-female transsexual patients. Significant increases were observed for venous thrombosis/ pulmonary embolism, depressive mood changes, hyperprolactinemia and elevated liver enzymes in the male-to-female transsexual patients. In the female-to-male group acne (12.3%) and weight increases > 10% (17.2%) were the main side effects. Many side effects were reversible with appropriate therapy or temporary discontinuation of hormones.

The occurrence of serious side effects (e.g., the prevalence of thromboembolic disease of 2.1% in patients below 40 years of age and 12% in patients above 40 years) was, however, not rare. In view of the needs of transsexuals these side effects present a difficult dilemma in hormonal gender reassignment. At present no firm guidelines can be given. The cornerstone of the decision to prescribe cross-gender hormones remains with the explanation of the possible side effects to the patients and careful clinical judgment.

Efforts to reduce the risk of thromboembolic events by transdermal administration of estrogen are very promising but not conclusive at this moment. Further follow-up of this relatively young population to disclose long-term side effects is required.

CONCLUSION

Hormones are indispensable tools for the induction and maintenance of the characteristics of the sex the transsexual reckons him/ herself to belong to. Following sex reassignment surgery they are hypogonadal and they must receive in principle lifelong hormone replacement in the same fashion as other hypogonadal patients. The main goal is to prevent future osteoporosis manifesting itself in the fifth and higher decades of their lives.

REFERENCES

Asscheman, H., Gooren, L.J.G. & Eklund, P.L.E. (1989). Mortality and morbidity in transsexual patients with cross-gender hormone treatment. Metabolism, 38, 869-873.

Conte, F.A., Grumbach, M.M., Kaplan, S.L. & Reiter, E.O. (1980). Correlation of LRH-induced LH and FSH release from infancy to 19 years with the changing pattern of gonadotropin secretion in agonadal patients: Relation to the restraint of puberty. Journal of Clinical Endocrinology and Metabolism, 50, 163-168.

Futterweit, W. (1980). Endocrine management of transsexuals. Hormonal profiles of serum prolactin, testosterone and estradiol. New York State Journal of Medicine, 80, 1260-1264.

Gooren, L.J.G., Assies, J., Asscheman, H., de Slegte, R. & van Kessel, H. (1988). Estrogen-induced prolactinoma in a man. Journal of Clinical Endocrinology and Metabolism, 66, 444-446.

Hamburger, C. (1969). Endocrine treatment of male and female transsexualism. In: Transsexualism and sex reassignment. Green, R. & Money, J. (eds), Baltimore, Johns Hopkins University Press, 291-307.

Leavitt, F., Berger, J.C., Hoepnerr, J.A. & Northop, G. (1980). Presurgical adjustment in male transsexuals with and without hormonal treatment. Journal of Nervous and Mental Diseases, 168, 693-697.

Meyer, W.J., Finkelstein, J.W., Stuart, C.A., Webb, A., Smith, E.R., Payer, A.F. & Walker, P.A. (1981). Physical and hormonal evaluation of transsexual patients during hormonal therapy. Archives of Sexual Behavior, 10, 347-356.

Meyer, W.J., Webb, A., Stuart, C.A., Finkelstein, J.W., Lawrence, B., Walker, P.A. (1986). Physical and hormonal evaluation of transsexual patients. A longitudinal study. Archives of Sexual Behavior, 15, 121-138.

Money, J. & Ambinder, R. (1978). Two year real life diagnostic test: Rehabilitation versus cure. In: Controversy in psychiatry. Brady, J.P. & Brody, H.K.M. (eds). Philadelphia, W.B. Saunders, 833-845.

The Influence of Hormone Treatment
on Psychological Functioning
of Transsexuals

Peggy T. Cohen-Kettenis, PhD
Louis J.G. Gooren, MD

SUMMARY. The effects of hormone treatment of transsexuals on the emotional state and sexual feelings have been studied less extensively than the effects on physical appearance and functioning. Most of the research in the field of hormone-behavior relationships has been carried out in non-patient groups or in patient groups other than transsexuals. Results of the few available studies of transsexuals are generally consistent with this research.

In the existing literature the following hormonal effects on sexuality are reported: an enhancement of sexual interest, fantasies and initiative after androgen administration in female-to-male transsexuals; a loss of sexual interest as well as a loss of erections and the capacity to reach orgasm in male-to-female transsexuals after the use of antiandrogens.

Less thoroughly investigated are the effects of hormone treatment on moods. In transsexuals, the following effects are reported: in male-to-female transsexuals less feelings of tension and more feelings of relaxation after anti-androgen intake and a calming down of emotional disturbances after estrogen intake; a greater sense of well-being in female-to-male transsexuals using androgens. No systematic effects of androgens on aggression and anger were found. Non-androgen factors appear to be more important determinants of aggression than androgens.

Peggy T. Cohen-Kettenis is affiliated with the Department of Child and Adolescent Psychiatry at the University Hospital, Utrecht. Louis J.G. Gooren is affiliated with the Department of Andrology/Endocrinology, Free University Hospital, Amsterdam.

INTRODUCTION

Once the diagnosis of transsexualism has sufficiently been established, patients enter the second stage of the gender reassignment procedure. This stage was first proposed by Money and Ambinder (1978) and is called the 'real-life diagnostic test.' Depending on the gender team involved sooner or later after entering the 'real life diagnostic test' hormone treatment is started.

The main physical effects of hormone treatment in male-to-female transsexuals are loss of body/pubic hair, reduction of scalp hair loss, reduction of testicular volume, loss of erections, induction of breast development and changes in body fat distribution due to estrogens (ethinylestradiol) and antiandrogens (cyproterone acetate). In female-to-male transsexuals androgen administration (mostly testosterone undecanoate or long-acting testosterone esters) results in deepening of the voice, facial and body hair growth, clitoral growth, and, in most cases, amenorrhea. If menstruation persists, lynestrenol (a progestative agent) is prescribed (Asscheman, 1989).

Entering this second phase of the treatment has, of course, a great impact on the emotional situation of the patients. Emotional imbalance can be caused by psychosocial factors (e.g., loss of friends), by indirect hormonal effects (e.g., subjects' responses to physical effects, like clitoris growth) and by direct hormonal effects (e.g., changes in sexual feelings). We will first discuss the psychosocial and indirect hormonal effects and then review the literature on direct hormonal effects.

At the time of their first appointment for gender problems most patients are very depressed. They have often tried to live according to their biological sex without success and suffer ensuing distress. When they decide to undergo sex reassignment surgery (SRS) as a solution to their gender problem, depressive feelings tend to diminish. But, despite the fact that one is looking forward to sex reassignment, other difficulties can emerge.

SRS involves a great deal of loss. There can be a loss of family contacts, friends, employment, housing and social status (Kuiper & Cohen-Kettenis, in press). Undergoing SRS implicates reorienting to the future in all of the aforementioned areas. During a certain amount of time, the transsexuals' changes of appearance provide a source of confusion. The ambiguity of the sex characteristics may lead to unpleasant (sometimes even aggressive) confrontations with strangers. Family and friends find it hard to adjust to the new situation. Even when trying to cooperate, family and friends keep using their given name or referring to the natal sex. In cases where family and friends do not accept the new situation, they often put pressure on the transsexual to abandon the goal of SRS. This is especially true for husbands, wives and children.

Building a new circle of friends during the real life test is not always easy, as one may find it hard to initiate contacts when the new gender role has not yet been completely established.

The physical changes, though very much desired, can also be psychologically difficult to handle for the transsexual. Some changes are not expected. Female-to-male transsexuals, for example, are often ashamed of their acne and their fluctuating voice while they also experience pain as their clitoris is enlarged. As for male-to-female transsexuals, even though their breast development is painful in the beginning, they feel it seldom takes place fast enough. Despite the use of antiandrogens, occasional erections still cause embarrassment or discomfort.

Complexities do not only arise because of undesired social consequences of the gender role change or hormonal (side) effects. Both female and male transsexuals are eager to engage in more intimate relationships. However, they often have avoided sexual contacts out of reluctance to reveal their transsexuality to others. As a confrontation with their own sexual body parts is very painful, they sometimes have repressed all sexual feelings and have sexually not been very active. Therefore, when they are sexually approached during the real life test, this can create approach-avoidance conflicts or it can even be a frightening experience.

Direct psychological and emotional effects of hormone therapy in transsexuals are not as well studied as the physical effects. Studies on hormone-emotion relationships have been carried out in other populations. The most extensively investigated areas are sexuality and aggression.

Sexuality. Some but not all aspects of sexuality appear to be influenced by androgens. In young boys as well as in older men, sexual activity and sexual function were associated with higher levels of testosterone (Davidson, Chen, Crapo, Gray, Greenleaf, & Catania, 1983; Tsitouras, Martin & Harman, 1982; Udry, Billy & Morris, 1984). In hypogonadal men testosterone therapy seemed to be of influence on sexual cognitive processes, like fantasizing (Bancroft & Wu, 1983; Gooren, 1987), but not on other aspects of sexual behavior like erections (Davidson, Camargo & Smith, 1979; Kwan, Greenleaf, Mann, Crapo & Davidson, 1983).

In the treatment of sex offenders surgical castration and administration of androgenic antagonists (cyproterone acetate or CPA) have been used to reduce levels of circulating testosterone as an attempt to establish a reduction in sexually offensive behavior. Castration appeared to have a highly variable effect on sexuality. Effects were very much dependent on age of castration (Heim, 1981). CPA proved to produce reductions in arousal and sexual activity, but not in erectile responses to erotic stimuli (Bradford, 1990; Marshall, Jones, Ward, Johnson, & Barbaree, 1991).

Recent studies have shown a comparable influence of androgens on female sexuality. In normally menstruating women, the midcycle testosterone level and/or the average testosterone level throughout the cycle were related to sexual desire, sexual interest and autoerotic behaviors, but less so to orgasmic frequency or coital frequency (Bancroft, 1987; Bancroft, Sanders, Davidson, & Warner, 1983; Persky, Charney, Lief, O'Brien, Miller, & Strauss, 1978). Surgically postmenopausal women taking androgens and women suffering from polycystic ovary syndrome and thus producing high levels of androgens, also showed an increased sexual interest and/or initiative (Gorzynski & Katz, 1977; Sherwin, 1985; Sherwin & Gelfand, 1984, 1985; Sitters-Zwolsman et al., 1987).

From the aforementioned studies the conclusion can be drawn that testosterone plays a major role in cognitive and motivational aspects of male as well as female sexuality.

The association between estrogen and aspects of sexual functioning has remained less clear. In normally cycling and postmenopausal women no relationships between sexual arousal, sexual fantasies, masturbation, initiation of sexual activity or coital frequency or sexual gratification and estradiol have been found (Abplanalp, Rose, Donnelly, & Livingston-Vaughan, 1979; Bancroft et al., 1983;

Leiblum, Bachmann, Kemmann, Colbum, & Schwartzman, 1983; Persky, Charney, Lief, O'Brien, Miller & Strauss, 1978). In several studies among surgically postmenopausal women, Sherwin (1988) found a decrease in sexual motivation after estradiol treatment while Dennerstein, Burrows, Wood, and Hyman (1980) and Dow, Hart, and Forrest (1983) found an enhancement of sexual functioning. The latter studies however have been criticized because of important methodological shortcomings (Sherwin, 1988). In sexually deviant males reduction of sexual drive has been reported after administration of estrogens (Whittaker, 1959).

The effect of estrogens on sexual functioning seems to be one of diminishing sexual interest instead of enhancement.

Aggression. Though well established in animal studies, evidence for an association between androgens and aggression is much more conflicting than for the relationship between androgens and sexuality.

Several measures of aggression and testosterone appeared to be related in adolescent and young men (Christiansen & Knussmann, 1987; Olweus, Mattsson, Schalling, & Low, 1980, 1988). Testosterone production and aggressive feelings were found not to be related in older men by Persky, Smith, and Basu (1971). Meyer-Bahlburg, Boon, Sharma, and Edward (1974) however could not replicate Persky et al.'s findings. Low and insignificant relations between self-report measures and plasma testosterone levels were also found in a longitudinal study (Doering, Brodie, Kraemer, Moos, Becker, & Mechanic, (1975)). No association between paper and pencil tests of aggression/hostility and testosterone levels were found by Brown and Davis (1975), Monti, Brown, and Corriveau (1977) and Rada, Kellner, and Winslow (1976).

In women, Persky et al. (1982) failed to find any association between hostility on the one hand and plasma levels of several androgens on the other hand. However Ehlers et al. (1980) found higher levels of testosterone in a female neurological outpatient population, who were selected on the basis of the incidence of violent behavior, when compared to a control group.

In men who actually committed sexually aggressive acts, both the presence and absence of a relationship between androgens and aggressive behavior has been reported (Bradford, 1990; Bradford

& Maclean, 1984; Hucker & Bain, 1990; Rada, Laws, Kellner, Striristava, & Peake, 1983).

Obviously a simple relationship between testosterone and aggression has not been found. Meta-analytic reviews show that women with their much lower testosterone levels than men are not always the less aggressive group. Factors like reactions and sex of the victim, guilt feelings or justification of the aggressive act account for differences in aggression between men and women (Eagly & Steffen, 1986; White, 1983). It may well be that such factors are more powerful predictors of aggression than androgens.

Moods. Men achieving a rise in status through their own efforts and having an elation of mood over the achievement, are likely to have a rise in testosterone (Mazur & Lamb, 1980). Testosterone administered to women deprived of ovarian androgen production induces a greater sense of well-being and fewer psychological symptoms than women from a control group experienced (Sherwin, 1985; Sherwin & Gelfand, 1984). In pubertal boys the emotional tone was higher than in prepubertal boys, while no such effects were found in girls (Crockett & Peterson, 1987). In one study, however, a negative correlation was found between rising testosterone levels and positive affect (Houser, 1979).

Estrogens seem to have a positive influence on mood disturbances. In women, psychiatric depression has been alleviated significantly as a consequence of treatment with high doses of estrogens (Vogel, Klaiber, & Broverman, 1978). Treatment with estrogens has sometimes been reported to be effective in women suffering from premenstrual syndrome or postpartum depressions (Astwood, 1970; O'Brien, 1987).

STUDIES INVOLVING TRANSSEXUALS

In two studies Leavitt, Berger, Hoeppner, and Northrop (1980) examined the effects of hormonal treatment on the adjustment of adult males requesting sex reassignment surgery. In the first study they compared Minnesota Multiphasic Personality Questionnaire (MMPI) profiles of 22 patients who received estrogen and medroxyprogesterone acetate for at least 12 months with profiles of 19 patients who received no hormonal therapy. They were all seeking presurgical psychiatric evaluation. Each patient was interviewed with the hormonal history carefully noted and given a battery of psychological tests including the MMPI. The reported hormone intake had resulted in breast development, testicular atrophy, skin smoothness, decreased rate of beard growth and no morning erections. Both groups were comparable in age and years of formal education.

Whereas the hormone group scored within the normal range on MMPI scales, the no-hormone group showed evidence of moderate disturbance in mood and thought, although they were not disturbed by psychiatric standards.

Factors other than hormones could, of course, have biased their findings (e.g., better adjustment in the hormone group, leading to initiation of hormone treatment, or living full-time as women in the hormone group). Therefore Leavitt et al. (1980) conducted a second study, which involved 20 male-to-female transsexuals undergoing hormonal treatment from 1 to 52 weeks. Weeks of hormonal treatment were evenly distributed over this period. There were no differences in age or education with the patient sample from the first study. Again the MMPI was administered to the patient group.

Length of full time cross-dressing appeared not to be associated with the patient's adjustment. The length of hormonal treatment however was associated with emotional adjustment on four clinical scales of the MMPI ('depression,' 'paranoia,' 'psychastenia' and 'faking good'). Leavitt et al. (1980) quote other authors who have observed 'sedative' (Hastings, 1969), 'calming' (Green, 1969) and 'bio-tranquilizing' (Block & Tessler, 1973) effects of estrogens in male-to-female transsexuals. They conclude that their study, in line with the aforementioned effects, strongly suggests a relationship between emotional adjustment and hormone therapy.

Recently Mallett et al. (1989) described a case of a male-to-female transsexual who developed a psychosis shortly after successful sex reassignment. In the literature, occasional cases of postoperative psychosis are explained in terms of a 'catastrophic psychological reaction to a complex and extraordinary set of events' (Mallett, Marshall, & Blacker 1989, p. 258). Although this might have been the case other explanations are also possible. The features of her illness were very similar to cases of 'puerperal' psychosis (psychosis shortly after childbirth). As estrogen treatment is usually interrupted a few weeks before surgery, the authors suspect that estrogen withdrawal could have played a causal role. The patient recovered shortly after estrogen treatment was reinstated. This publication led to another report on a similar case by Faulk (1989).

The influence of RU 23.903 (Anandron, a pure antiandrogen) on sexual functioning, aggression and mood was studied by Van Kemenade, Cohen-Kettenis, Cohen and Gooren (1989) in a group of 14 male-to-female presurgical transsexuals. The morning before hormone treatment was started, the patients were given a test battery. After 8 weeks, a second test procedure was performed. The patients were asked to fill out two tests each day at home, namely the Visual Analogue Mood Scale (VAMS; Zeally & Aitken, 1969) and a Sex Diary (Bancroft et al., 1983). The latter test consists of items on nocturnal and morning erections, thoughts and fantasies about sex, masturbation, erections during the day, orgasm, coitus, perceived extent of libido, excitement and orgasm. As part of the test battery, aggression was measured by the Dutch Spielberger Trait-State-Anger Scale (Van der Ploeg, Defares & Spielberger, 1982) and the VAMS (Zeally & Aitken, 1969).

Only morning erections and frequencies of sexual thoughts and sexual (but not other) fantasies decreased after antiandrogen intake. Aggression/anger was not affected by changes in testosterone level. Lowering testosterone levels also corresponded with positive affect, as feelings of relaxation and level of energy became stronger while tension/anxiety and fatigue were decreasing after Anandron intake.

Preliminary findings of a similar study in female-to-male transsexuals suggest that androgen intake increases sexual motivation and arousability. No effects were found in the area of anger and aggression (Van Goozen, Cohen-Kettenis, Gooren & Van de Poll, in prep).

Summarizing the above findings one can say that in female-to-male transsexuals androgen administration during the real-life test will considerably enhance their sexual interest, fantasies and initiative. Sherwin (1988) has postulated that fluctuations in exposure to androgens instead of absolute levels are responsible for the greater sensitivity in women than in men. According to this theory the prominence of sexual thoughts and interest should be high in the first weeks after hormone treatment, but should diminish as soon as stable elevated androgen levels are established. In the first few months after androgen intake, clitoris growth may be another reason for preoccupation with sexuality.

In male-to-females the use of antiandrogens as well as estrogens may result in loss of sexual interest as well as loss of erections and the capacity to reach orgasm.

From the literature the effects of androgens on aggression are still unclear. Also little is known of the interaction between falling (or rising) estrogen levels and rising (or falling) androgen levels in the female-to-male (or male-to-female) group.

In non-transsexual populations, positive as well as negative influences of androgens on mood have been reported. In male-to-female transsexuals, antiandrogens appeared to have different effects on various moods. For instance, feelings of relaxation, fatigue, tension and anxiety as well as level of energy fluctuated more as a consequence of antiandrogen intake than cheerfulness, sociability, gloominess and irritation. For female-to-male transsexuals no such data are available yet. On the basis of studies in non-transsexual groups, an enhanced sense of well-being could be expected after androgen intake.

As the main effect of estrogens seems to be one of calming down emotional turbulences, those male-to-female transsexuals who are emotionally very unstable are likely to benefit most from estrogen therapy.

Psychologically the real life test is a complicated phase in the SRS procedure. Many internal and social changes undoubtedly imply emotional disturbances. Hormone therapy seems to be an extra factor, not only because the hormones embody a fulfillment of a desperate wish but also because the hormones themselves influence emotions.

Results of the first studies on transsexuals are quite consistent with the general literature on hormone-emotion relationships. However most of the studies suffer from methodological flaws. The samples sizes are usually small, moods/emotions are operationalized in diverse ways and adequate control groups are lacking.

Moreover female-to-male transsexuals are hardly studied. Long term studies on psychological and emotional effects of hormone treatment have not yet appeared in print (to the best of our knowledge).

As other patient groups usually get much lower doses of sex hormones than transsexuals, more hormone studies in transsexuals are called for. Information coming from such research would constitute a significant step forward towards an adequate treatment of transsexuals.

REFERENCES

Abplanalp, J. M., Rose, R. M., Donnelly, A. F., & Livingston-Vaughan, L. (1979). Psychoendocrinology of the menstrual cycle: II. The relationship between enjoyment of activities, moods, and reproductive hormones. *Psychosomatic Medicine, 41,* 605-615.

Asscheman, H. (1989). *Cross-gender hormone treatment; side effects and some metabolic aspects.* Amsterdam, Huisdrukkerij Vrije Universiteit.

Astwood, E. B. (1970). Estrogens and progestins. In L. S. Goodman & A. Gilman (Eds.) *The Pharmacological Basis of Therapeutics.* Toronto: Macmillan Co.

Bancroft, J. (1987). Hormones, sexuality and fertility in humans. *Journal of Zoology, 213,* 445-461.

Bancroft, J., Sanders, D., Davidson, D., & Warner, P. (1983). Mood, sexuality, hormones and the menstrual cycle: III. Sexuality and the role of androgens. *Psychosomatic Medicine, 45,* 509-516.

Bancroft, J., & Wu, F. C. W. (1983). Changes in erectile responsiveness during androgens. *Psychosomatic Medicine, 45,* 509-516.

Block, N. L., & Tessler, A. N. (1973). Transsexualism and surgical procedures. *Medical aspects of human sexuality, 7,* 158-181.

Bradford, J. M. W. (1990). The antiandrogen and hormonal treatment of sex offenders. In W. L. Marshall, D. R. Laws & H. E. Barbaree (Eds.) *Handbook of sexual assault.* New York: Plenum Press.

Bradford, J. M. W., & Maclean, D. (1984). Sexual offenders, violence and testosterone: A chemical study. *Canadian Journal of Psychiatry, 29,* 335-343.

Brown, W., & Davis, G. (1975). Serum testosterone and irritability in man. *Psychosomatic Medicine, 37,* 87.

Christiansen, K., & Knussmann, R. (1987). Androgen levels and components of aggressive behavior in men. *Hormones and Behavior, 21,* 2, 170-180.

Crockett, L. J., & Peterson, A. C. (1987). Pubertal status and psychosocial development: findings from the early adolescence study. In R. M. Lerner & T. T. Foch (Eds.) *Biological-psychological interactions in early adolescence.* Hillsdale: Erlbaum.

Davidson, J. M., Camargo, C. A., & Smith E. R. (1979). Effects of androgen on sexual behavior in hypogonadal men. *Journal of Clinical Endocrinology and Metabolism, 48,* 955-958.

Davidson, J. M., Chen, J. J., Crapo, L., Gray, D., Greenleaf, W. J., & Catania, J. A. (1983). Hormonal changes and sexual functioning in aging men. *Journal of Clinical Endocrinology and Metabolism, 57,* 71-77.

Dennerstein, L., Burrows, G. D., Wood, C., & Hyman, G. (1980). Hormones and sexuality: Effect of estrogen and progesterone. *Obstetrics and gynecology, 56,* 316-322.

Doering, C., Brodie, J., Kraemer, H., Moos, R., Becker, H., & Mechanic, D. (1975). Negative affect and plasma testosterone: A longitudinal human study. *Psychosomatic Medicine, 37,* 484-491.

Dow, M. G. T., Hart, D. M., & Forrest, C. A. (1983). Hormonal treatments of sexual unresponsiveness in postmenopausal women: A comparative study. *British Journal of Obstetrics and Gynecology, 90,* 361-366.

Eagly, A. H., & Steffen, V. J. (1986). Gender and aggressive behavior: A meta-analytic review of the social psychological literature. *Psychological Bulletin, 100,* 309-330.

Ehlers, C. L., Rickler, K. C., & Hovey, J. E. (1980). A possible relationship between plasma testosterone and aggressive behavior in a female outpatient population. In M. Girgin & I. G. Kiloh (Eds.) *Limbic Epilepsy and Dyscontrol Syndrome.* Amsterdam, Elsevier.

Faulk, M. (1989). Psychosis in a transsexual. *British Journal of Psychiatry, 156,* 285-286.

Gooren, L. J. G. (1987). Androgen levels and sex functions in testosterone-treated hypogonadal men. *Archives of Sexual Behavior, 16,* 463-473.

Gorzynski, G., & Katz, J. L., (1977). The polycystic ovary syndrome: Psychosexual correlates. *Archives of Sexual Behavior, 6,* 215-222.

Green, R. (1969). Psychiatric management of special problems in transsexualism. In R. Green & J. Money (Eds.) *Transsexualism and sex reassignment.* Baltimore: Johns Hopkins Press.

Hastings, D. W. (1969). Inauguration of a research project on transsexualism in a university medical center. In. R. Green & J. Money (Eds.) *Transsexualism and sex reassignment.* Baltimore: Johns Hopkins Press.

Heim, N. (1981). Sexual behavior of castrated sex offenders. *Archives of Sexual Behavior, 10,* 11-19.

Houser, B. (1979). An investigation of the correlation between hormonal levels in males and mood, behavior and physical discomfort. *Hormones and behavior, 12,* 185-197.

Hucker, S. J., & Bain J. (1990). Androgenic hormones and sexual assault. In W. L. Marshall, D. R. Laws & H. E. Barbaree (Eds.) *Handbook of sexual assault.* New York: Plenum Press.

Kwan, M., Greenleaf, J., Mann, J., Crapo, L., & Davidson, J. M. (1983). The nature of androgen action on male sexuality: A combined laboratory-self-report study on hypogonadal men. *Journal of Clinical Endocrinology and Metabolism, 57,* 557-562.

Leavitt, F., Berger, J. C., Hoeppner, J., & Northrop, G. (1980). Presurgical adjustment in male transsexuals with and without hormonal treatment. *Journal of Nervous and Mental Disease, 168,* 693-697.

Leiblum, S., Bachmann, G., Kemmann, E., Colburn, D., & Schwartzman, L. (1983). Vaginal atrophy in the postmenopausal women: The importance of sexual activity and hormones. *Journal of the American Medical Association, 249,* 2195-2198.

Mallet, P., Marshall, E. J., & Blacker C. V. R. (1989). 'Puerperal psychosis' following male-to-female sex reassignment? *British Journal of Psychiatry, 155,* 257-259.

Marshall W. L., Jones, R., Ward, T., Johnson P., & Barbaree, H.E. (1991). Treatment outcome with sex offenders. *Clinical Psychology Review,* 11, 465-485.

Mazur, A., & Lamb, T. A. (1980). Testosterone, status and mood in human males. *Hormones and Behavior, 14,* 236-246.

Meyer-Bahlburg, H., Boon, D. A., Sharma, M., & Edward, J. A. (1974). Aggressiveness and testosterone measures in man. *Psychosomatic Medicine, 36,* 269-274.

Money, J., & Ambinder, R. (1978). Two-year, real-life diagnostic test: rehabilitation versus cure. In J. P. Brady & H. K. H. Brodie (Eds.) *Controversy in Psychiatry.* Philadelphia: Saunders.

Monti, P., Brown, W., & Corriveau, D. (1977). Testosterone and components of aggressive and sexual behavior in man. *American Journal of Psychiatry, 134,* 962-964.

O'Brien, P. M. S. (1987). *Premenstrual syndrome.* Oxford: Blackwell Scientific Publications.

Olweus, D., Mattsson, A., Schalling, D., & Low, H. (1980). Testosterone, aggression, physical, and personality dimensions in normal adolescent males. *Psychosomatic Medicine, 42,* 253-268.

Olweus, D., Mattsson, A., Schalling, D., & Low, H. (1988). Circulating testosterone levels and aggression in adolescent males: a causal analysis. *Psychosomatic Medicine, 50,* 261-272.

Persky, H., Charney, N., Lief, H. I., O'Brien, C. P., Miller, W. R. & Strauss, D. (1978). The relationship of plasma estradiol level to sexual behavior in young women. *Psychosomatic Medicine, 40,* 523-535.

Persky, H., Dreisbach, L., Miller, W. R., O'Brien, C. P., Khan, M. A., Lief, H. I., & Strauss, D. (1982). The relation of plasma androgen levels to sexual behaviors and attitudes of women. *Psychosomatic Medicine, 44,* 305-319.

Persky, H., Smith, K. D., & Basu, G. K. (1971). Relation of psychological measures of aggression and hostility to testosterone production in man. *Psychological Medicine, 33,* 265-277.

Rada, R., Kellner, R., & Winslow, W. (1976). Plasma testosterone and aggressive behavior. *Psychosomatics, 17,* 138-142.

Rada, R., Laws, D., Kellner, R., Striristava, L., & Peake, G. (1983). Plasma androgens in violent and non-violent sex offenders. *Bulletin of the American Academy of Psychiatry and Law, 11*, 149-158.

Sherwin, B. B. (1985). Changes in sexual behavior as a function of plasma sex steroid levels in post-menopausal women. *Maturitas, 7*, 225-233.

Sherwin B. B., & Gelfand, M. M., (1984). Effects of parenteral administration of estrogen and androgen on plasma hormone levels and hot flushes in the surgical menopause. *American Journal of Obstetrics and Gynecology, 148*, 552-557.

Sherwin, B. B., & Gelfand, M. M. (1985). Differential symptom response to parenteral estrogen and/or androgen administration in the surgical menopause. *American Journal of Obstetrics and Gynecology, 151*, 153-160.

Sherwin, B. B. (1988). A comparative analysis of the role of androgen in human male and female sexual behavior: Behavioral specificity, critical thresholds, and sensitivity. *Psychobiology, 16*, 416-425.

Sitters-Zwolsman, C. M., Boer, K., Cohen-Kettenis, P. T., De Jonge, F. H., Hamerlynck, J. V. TH, Hogerzeil, H. V., Van de Poll, N. E. (1987). Aggressive and sexual behavior in adult women with high levels of testosterone. In A. M. L. Coenen & J. M. H. Vossen (Eds.) *Comparative and Physiological Psychology*. Nijmegen: De Witte Studentenpers.

Tsitouras, P. D., Martin, C. E., & Harman, S. M. (1982). Relationship of serum testosterone to sexual activity in healthy elderly men. *Journal of Gerontology, 37*, 288-293.

Udry, J. R., Billy, J. O., & Morris, N. M. (1984). Serum androgenic hormones motivate sexual behavior in adolescent boys. *Fertility and sterility, 42*, 683-685.

Van der Ploeg, H. M., Defares, P. B., & Spielberger, C. D. (1982). *Handleiding bij de zelfanalysevragenlijst, ZAV. Een vragenllijst voor het meten van boosheid en woede, als toestand en als dispositie. Een nederlandstalige bewerking van de Spielberger State-Trait Anger Scale (The Dutch translation of the Spielberger State-Trait Anger Scale)*. Lisse, The Netherlands: Swetz & Zeitlinger.

Van Goozen, S. H. M., Cohen-Kettenis, P. T., Gooren, L. J. G., & Van de Poll, N. E. (in prep.) The influence of androgens on aggression, anger tendency, sexual motivation and cognitive abilities: A questionnaire study in female-to-male transsexuals.

Van Kemenade, J. F. L. M., Cohen-Kettenis, P. T., Cohen, L., & Gooren, L. J. G. (1989). Affects of the pure antiandrogen RU 23.903 (Anandron) on sexuality, aggression, and mood in male-to-female transsexuals. *Archives of Sexual Behavior, 18*, 217-227.

Vogel, W., Klaiber, E. L., & Broverman D. M. (1978). Roles of the gonadal steroid hormones in psychiatric depression in men and women. *Progress in Neuropsychopharmacology, 2*, 487-503.

White, J. W. (1983). Sex and gender issues in aggression research. *Aggression, 2*, 1-26.

Whittaker, L. H. (1959). Oestrogens and psychosexual disorders. *Medical Journal of Australia, 2*, 547-549.

Zeally, A. K., & Aitken, R. C. B. Measurement of mood (1969). *Proceedings of Research in Social Medicine, 62*, 933-996.

Regrets After Sex Reassignment Surgery

Friedemann Pfäfflin, MD

SUMMARY. Using data drawn from the follow-up literature covering the last 30 years, and the author's clinical data on 295 men and
women after SRS, an estimation of the number of patients who regretted the operations is made. Among female-to-male transsexuals
after SRS, i.e., in men, no regrets were reported in the author's sample, and in the literature they amount to less than 1%. Among male-
to-female transsexuals after SRS, i.e., in women, regrets are reported
in 1-1.5%. Poor differential diagnosis, failure to carry out the real-
life-test, and poor surgical results seem to be the main reasons behind the regrets reported in the literature. According to three cases
observed by the author in addition to personality traits the lack of
proper care in treating the patients played a major role.

In the follow-up literature on transsexuals one widely used criterion is whether the patients regretted having undergone SRS. Considering the fact that, once SRS has been performed, a *restitutio ad
integrum* is no longer possible, regrets are a tragic outcome. Due to
the dearth of systematic research on contraindications for this specific treatment one would, therefore, prefer solid data on the actual
ratio of regrets instead of vague hints as they are often found in
general literature on transsexualism. Without quoting the authors,
Sigusch et al. (1979) for instance reported that at the Fifth International Gender Dysphoria Symposium, February 10-13, 1977, Nor-
folk, Va., it had been said, that a total of 44 patients had regretted
SRS and wanted to return to their former gender role.

So far there have been two studies which have investigated re-

---

Dr. Friedemann Pfäfflin is Consultant Psychiatrist and Psychoanalyst, Ulm
University Clinic, Dept. of Psychotherapy, Am Hochsträss 8, 7900 Ulm, Germany.

grets within larger samples. Wålinder et al. (1978) found four regrets among the approximately one hundred persons who, up till July 1st, 1972, when the specific Swedish law came into force, had successfully applied to the Swedish authorities for permission to change their name and undergo possible further measures for sex reassignment. Four of these, three biological men and one biological woman, regretted the measures taken, although none had had SRS, but only hormonal treatment and change of name. In addition to this sample the authors described two biological men from the sample of Wålinder u. Thuwe (1975) who had had SRS, and three more cases, without however giving detailed information on how far their treatment had proceeded.

Blanchard et al. (1989) investigated 61 biological females and 50 biological males after SRS. Their annually administered questionnaire included two items: (1) If you have had a vaginoplasty or mastectomy, how do you feel about this operation now? (2) At the present time, do you feel that you would rather live as man or as woman? While none of the biological females showed regrets, four biological males, who, according to the authors belonged to the subgroup of heterosexual transsexuals, did so. None of them had however fully reverted to the male gender role.

Apart from these two studies, there are a number of case reports, which cannot however be used to gauge the ratio or frequency of regrets. For this purpose, larger samples are a prerequisite. The following study relies on two such samples: (1) cumulative numbers from follow-up studies, and (2) own clinical sample.

Regret, in this study, is defined as *gender dysphoria in the new gender role and after SRS which is expressed in behavior*, i.e., attempts at re-reorientation of gender role behavior and/or re-adoption of the former sex/gender-role behavior and/or applications for legal name/gender change and/or attempts to have SRS reversed.

In contrast to the linguistic usage in most of the literature on transsexualism, the term *(male-to-female or female-to-male) transsexual* is used for gender dysphoric and transsexual patients *before* SRS, whereas patients *after* SRS are addressed according to their *new* gender role, i.e., as women (former male-to-female-transsexuals) or men (former female-to-male transsexuals). From a clinical point of view and considering the problems of rehabilitation it seems essential to drop the medical diagnosis as soon as possible and to address patients according to the gender role they live in. Once gender reorientation, change of Christian name and legal change of sex have taken place it seems anachronistic and anything but helpful for the patient to talk in diagnostic terms or in terms of *biological* sex. We prefer this linguistic usage, as it seems to help the integration of the patients in the new gender role, even though in the context of regrets it may complicate the matter.

SAMPLES

Sample 1

Sample 1 includes 74 follow-up studies and 8 reviews, published between 1961 and 1991. Only those reports which referred to at least a minimum of 5 patients after SRS have been included. More than half of the 74 follow-up studies described samples from the U.S.A. (n = 36), 13 German, 7 Swedish, 6 Swiss, 5 British, 4 Danish, 3 Canadian and Australian samples respectively, 2 Dutch, and 1 from Finland, Norway and Singapore respectively. Most of the studies were conducted at psychiatric university clinics or at surgical, urological or gynecological departments of university clinics. Some studies were joint ventures by psychiatrists and/or surgeons and/or endocrinologists. Some of the studies came from specific treatment units as, e.g., Gender Identity Clinics and the like. Very few studies came from general hospitals or private practices who, in most cases, cooperated with research foundations such as the Harry Benjamin Research Foundation.

The following studies were included: Hertz et al. 1961, Benjamin 1964 a,b,c, 1966, 1967, Pomeroy 1967, Wålinder 1967, Money and Brennan 1968, Money and Primrose 1968, Vogt 1968, Walser 1968, Fogh-Andersen 1969, Randell 1969, Hoenig et al. 1970 a,b, Money and Ehrhardt 1970, Alanko and Achté 1971, Hoenig et al. 1971, Money 1971, Jones 1972, Arieff 1973, Edgerton and Meyer 1973, Gandy 1973, Ihlenfeld 1973, Kando 1973, Hastings 1974, Laub and Fisk 1974, Hore et al. 1975, Wålinder and Thuwe 1975, McKee 1976, Steiner 1976, Stürup 1976, Stone 1977, Tsoi et al. 1978,

Hastings and Markland 1978, Jayaram et al. 1978, König et al. 1978, Turner et al. 1978, Wålinder et al. 1978, Wyler 1978, Meyer and Reter 1979, Wyler et al. 1979, Hunt and Hampson 1980, Lothstein 1980, Spengler 1980, Zingg et al. 1980, Ball 1981, Kröhn et al. 1981, Lundström et al. 1981, Sörensen 1981 a,b, Eicher 1983, Simona-Politta 1983, Eicher 1984, McCauley and Ehrhardt 1984, Wiegand 1984, Blanchard et al. 1985, Kuiper 1985, Lindemalm et al. 1986, McEwan et al. 1986, Blanchard et al. 1987, Fahrner et al. 1987, Junge 1987, Kockott and Fahrner 1988, Kuiper and Cohen-Kettenis 1988, Täschner and Wiesbeck 1988, Dudle 1989, Herms 1989, Ross and Need 1989, Wiesbeck and Täschner 1989, Mate-Kole et al. 1990, Pfäfflin and Junge 1990, Stein et al. 1990, Eicher et al. 1991.

The reviews were by Pauly 1965, 1968, 1974 a,b, 1981, Lothstein 1982, Abramowitz 1986, Green and Fleming 1990.

Due to various kinds of overlap between the samples it is not possible to determine the exact total number of patients after SRS included in these studies (cp. Pfäfflin & Junge 1992, who give a detailed evaluation of these follow-ups and reviews). In a very rough approximation they add up to some 1.000 to 1.600 women (i.e., male-to-female) and 400 to 550 men (i.e., female-to-male transsexuals).

Sample 2

Sample 2 consists of gender dysphoric and transsexual patients the author has treated irregularly or regularly and for shorter or longer periods since 1978. Some of them had had SRS as early as the late forties and early fifties but were still coming for irregular consultations. Taking the key-date of March 31st, 1992, these were 616 patients, 449 male-to-female and 167 female-to-male transsexuals (ratio 3.74:1). Of these a total of 297 had had SRS, 196 male-to-female transsexuals, now women, and 99 female-to-male transsexuals, now men (ratio 1.97:1), with a minimum follow-up time after SRS of one year and a maximum of 29 years (except for two women who were operated within the last nine months; for further details compare the extensive follow-up of subsamples of 42 women and 43 men, conducted in 1984-86, Junge 1987, Pfäfflin

& Junge 1990). In line with the findings of other researchers in our sample the male group of gender dysphoric patients is much more heterogeneous than the female group; this accounts for the differences in the proportions between operated and not-operated patients in both groups.

RESULTS

Sample 1

Adding all regrets from the follow-up literature mentioned above, there are twenty women (Hertz et al. 1961, Benjamin 1966, Walser 1968, Randell 1969, Alanko & Achté 1971, Hastings 1974, Wålinder & Thuwe 1975, Stürup 1976, Wålinder et al. 1978, Ball 1981, Kröhn et al. 1981, Lindemalm et al. 1986), and five men (Benjamin 1966, Money & Ehrhardt 1970, König et al. 1978, Meyer & Reter 1979, McCauley & Ehrhardt 1970). Since, as mentioned before, due to overlap between the samples, it is impossible to determine the sum total, it is also impossible, to give exact percentages (estimation for men < 1%, for women 1-1.5%). Where the follow-up literature contains case histories one can however look into these cases more closely.

Regrets in men. It seems highly probable that one of the five patients is mentioned twice (Money & Ehrhardt 1970, Meyer & Reter 1979). He had evaded the regulations of the Gender Identity Clinic and got a phalloplasty elsewhere, the results of which were disastrous, despite several attempts to improve them. He was a suicidal drug-addict living alternatingly as a man or a woman. According to Meyer and Reter (1979) he just wanted to have the phalloplasty removed, but did not question the other steps connected with sex reassignment.

Information on the other three patients is sparse. They all regretted the operation (or operations?). In one case nothing is known about any behavioral consequences (König et al. 1978); one returned to his former female gender-role behavior (McCauley & Ehrhardt 1984); the last had SRS without completing a real-life-test beforehand and could not manage to live as a man; he later had a mammoplasty (Benjamin 1966).

Regrets in women. Two of the twenty women are mentioned twice (Wålinder & Thuwe 1975, Wålinder et al. 1978). Two further patients had only started hormonal treatment; one of them underwent a religious conversion (Hastings 1974), the other one developed a paranoid psychosis and committed suicide (Stürup 1976); but neither had had SRS; they do not therefore meet the criteria for regret, mentioned above. Two other patients returned only temporarily and occasionally to their former male behavior (Ball 1981, Kröhn et al. 1981), the one extensively described by Ball (1981) being threatened with the loss of his claims to a large inheritance and an aristocratic title if he showed up as a woman. Benjamin (1966), finally, mentioned a patient who *considered* returning to a life as a man but does not provide any information whether she/he actually did so.

Investigating the remaining 14 cases, there are three factors that essentially contribute to regrets: (1) aspects of *differential-diagnostic indications for SRS*, (2) closely linked to this, the *extent to which the real-life-test has been successfully tried out*, and (3) the *extent and quality of surgical measures.*

At least four patients developed *psychoses or paranoid reactions* (Hertz et al. 1961, Alanko & Achté 1971, Hastings 1974, Wålinder & Thuwe 1978), and one might ask if these developments could not have been foreseen, had the patients been in continuous psychiatric treatment for long enough before the operation. The patient described by Hastings (1974) for instance in no way met the generally accepted criteria for SRS; he had a history of violent criminal behavior, was an alcoholic, had cut his penis with a razor-blade and later on castrated himself, and finally by threatening suicide, coerced the surgeons into carrying out a vaginoplasty. One of the patients described by Stürup (1976) had also attempted autocastration several times, behavior which, according to Springer's review (1981), diagnostically generally points into the direction of psychosis rather than transsexualism. His treatment was contradictory: he first was given male hormones, and later female hormones. He was castrated, but did not have a vaginoplasty. The patient had kept secret the fact that he was married, which meant he could not apply for a legal name change, and had to live as a woman with a male identity card. At the time of the follow-up, 19 years later, he was living as a man, but was still convinced that the operation had been necessary and only regretted that it had taken place so late.

At least three patients had not even attempted the *real-life-test* and were operated without having any experience as to how life as a woman would be (Walser 1968, Alanko & Achté 1961). One might add to this group the above mentioned psychotic patient described by Hastings (1974).

As a third essential factor that can lead to regrets, the authors mention *failure to make use of the surgical procedures available, and unsatisfactory surgical outcome of SRS.* Two patients had only orchidectomy with the penis being left in its place as it was. They had not been given a vaginoplasty and had become embittered that this was all they could achieve (Walser 1968, Stürup 1976). Others had to wait up to five years between orchidectomy and/or penectomy on the one hand, and vaginoplasty on the other hand (Hertz et al. 1961, Alanko & Achté 1971). Wherever surgical results are described in detail in the follow-up literature, they were, apart from a very few exceptions, deficient (e.g., Hertz et al. 1961, Benjamin 1966, Randell 1969, Wålinder & Thuwe 1975, Lindemalm et al. 1986).

Sample 2

Regrets in men. None of the 99 men expressed regrets.

Regrets in women. Three of the 196 women expressed regrets (1.53%). They had had SRS in 1974, 1983 and 1987, two of them in Germany and one in Casablanca, Morocco, and came for advice to our department in 1980, 1985 and 1991, i.e., six, two and four years after the operation. Only one of the patients had been in treatment with us before the operation. Two of them applied to the courts to have their former name change and/or legal sex change re-reverted in line with the regulations laid down in the German Law on Transsexuals, in force since January 1st, 1981 (Pfäfflin 1981, Augstein 1992, Will 1992). The third patient, who had been operated on in 1974 and come for counselling in 1980, had not had a legal name/sex change that could be re-reverted, since at that time the law did not provide such possibilities for transsexuals.

Looking for common factors in their biographies there are various areas that are worth mentioning. *Family background*: All three came from difficult family backgrounds with either broken homes, the early death of father or mother, or divorce and remarriage of parents, with parents who reacted with outrage and severely humiliated them (battering the children, calling them sissies, calling them by girls' names, making demonstrative suicide attempts, alcohol addiction, attempts of father to pander the son with the stepmother, etc.). Traumata connected with separation played a central role in all three biographies. *Onset of transvestite or transsexual behavior*: One of the three was cross-dressing before the age of ten years, the other two only from puberty onwards. Cross-dressing was combined with masturbation in a transvestite manner, but none of the patients had disclosed that to their physicians before SRS. *Sexual experience and partners*: None of them had had sex with boys or men before SRS. All had had long lasting partnerships with women, two were married (one even twice) and had fathered children. Two of the female partners came from foreign cultures and did not speak German so that the patients had to learn a new native tongue to be able to communicate with their partners. One of the female partners committed suicide, another one had just lost a former friend by suicide before she met the patient. After SRS one patient lost a male fiancé by suicide.

Treatment. All three patients had successfully lived in the female gender-role (real-life-test) prior to surgery for between one and four years, but none of them had been seen regularly by a psychiatrist prior to SRS. Two had been in more or less irregular treatment with psychologists and psychotherapists, both for less than ten months before they were sent to a clinic to have surgery. One of them had attended group sessions for transsexuals led by a psychologist which, retrospectively, he characterized as superficial conversation sessions. The patient I had sent to the surgeon after I had known him for 15 months had cancelled most of the appointments and had convinced me in a charming manner that he was doing very well as a woman and was so weighed down by his new business that he just could not afford the time to come to the appointments until I finally gave up insisting on further meetings. Hormonal treatment had been started by two of the patients without consulting a doctor, and by the third after having been seen five or six times by a psychotherapist. At the start of hormonal treatment the patients were 27, 30 and 39 years of age, at SRS they were 34, 32, and 39 years. The results of SRS were aesthetically and functionally good, with only one patient having a urethral-vaginal fistula which later on was successfully reoperated.

Analysing the object-relationships of the patients the predominant factor seemed to be a sado-masochistic structure, however without any overt sado-masochistic sexual behavior. Suicidal ideation and identification with the aggressor alternated with impulses of phantasised triumphant revenge to overcome their rage at their primary objects and later partners (Stoller 1975, Money 1986). Ego-structure and defense mechanisms were labile, and in periods of distress two of the patients displayed polyneurotic symptoms, including drug and alcohol abuse, and severe anxiety which diagnostically might best fit in with the borderline-structure (Kernberg 1975). After two to six years of having lived successfully as women all three patients returned to their former gender role behavior when their deeply rooted separation fears had been reactivated by their partners threatening to or actually leaving them. Two of them intermediately displayed overt psychotic and paranoid behavior. One was hospitalized and given neuroleptic treatment for some months. One became psychotic only within the therapeutic relationship, which confirms the borderline diagnosis. For a short time, they all considered having the SRS reversed, but, after extensive counselling, were able to give up the idea again.

All three patients are now living socially as men, hiding their breasts under loose-cut clothes, just as female-to-male transsexuals use to do. They regret SRS, but at the same time are convinced that they did not have any alternative when they actually underwent the operation. They describe it as a necessary step in their development which has given them insights they otherwise would never have achieved.

DISCUSSION

Wålinder et al. (1978) identified 13 unfavorable prognostic factors: Psychotic reactions, mental retardation, unstable personality, alcoholism-drug addiction, criminality, inadequacy in self-support, inadequate support from family, excessive geographical distance to treatment unit, physical build inappropriate to the new sex role, completion of military service, heterosexual experience, strong sexual interest, and higher age at request for intervention. In cases where the patients regretted the operation they found on average 7 to 8 such items (median 7.0, range 6-11) as opposed to the group of patients with favorable outcome (on average 2.8 factors, median 2.0, range 1 to 7). This difference was statistically significant (p < .02, Mann-Whitney, two-tail).

Blanchard et al. (1989) found statistically significantly more regrets among the subgroup of male-to-female transsexuals which they classified as heterosexual as opposed to homosexual.

In a literature survey of follow-up studies covering thirty years Pfäfflin & Junge (1992) found three major causes for regrets: (1) poor differential diagnostic procedures, (2) failure to carry out the real-life-test, and (3) disappointing surgical outcome.

From a clinical point of view it seems that transsexual patients suffer from many forms of minor regret after SRS. Pain during or after the operation, surgical complications, poor surgical results, loss of partners, loss of job, conflicts with families, disappointments that various expectations linked to SRS were not fulfilled–there are countless reasons for regrets. Usually such regrets are *temporary*. Most of them are realistically overcome after some time with or without the help of counsellors. The definition of regret as used in this paper does not apply to these forms of minor regret. As Kuiper (1985) and Cohen-Kettenis and Kuiper (1988) have shown, quite a few postoperative transsexuals suffer from various kinds of dysphoria, just as other people do, yet they no longer attribute their dysphoria to *gender* dysphoria. The number of lasting regrets which are attributed to *gender* dysphoria and expressed in behavior is small. In men (former female-to-male transsexuals) who seem to be a diagnostically more homogeneous group, they are less than 1%, in women (former male-to-female transsexuals) they range between 1 to 1.5%.

In whatever way one may explain transsexualism in terms of aetiology, it seems obvious that there is a continuum from sporadic episodes of gender dysphoric thoughts to stable cross gender identity experience and behavior, supporting the notion that transsexual behavior is a form of more or less successful and stable behavior which serves to defend the self against phantasized or real trauma. Psychiatric diagnosis and treatment aims at distinguishing between those cases where, in all probability, hormonal and surgical treatment will further stabilize the patient, and those cases where it will not. One way of avoiding regrets is to stick to the Standards of Care laid down by the International Harry Benjamin Gender Dysphoria Association, Inc. (Walker et al. 1985), which, alas, are not respected by many professionals who work in the field of transsexualism, and which the patients often try to circumvent because they misunderstand such standards as obstacles instead of support.

If one wants to avoid regrets it is vital to look at the patient's personality and behavioral traits. With this in mind, preventing regrets will entail focusing on the diagnostic and therapeutic procedures. Behavioral traits and the patient's personality are however nothing but conditions or prerequisites for later regrets; the responsibility lies with the psychologists, endocrinologists, psychiatrists and surgeons who switch the points in the direction of SRS.

REFERENCES

Abramowitz, S. (1986). Psychosocial Outcomes of Sex Reassignment Surgery. *Journal of Consulting and Clinical Psychology, 54*, 183-189.

Alanko, A., & Achté, K. (1971). Transsexualism. *Psychiatrica Fennica, 343-358*

Arieff, A. J. (1973). Five-Year Studies of Transsexuals: Psychiatric, Psychological, and Surgical Aspects. In L. D. Laub & P. Gandi (Eds.), *Proceedings of the Second Interdisciplinary Symposium on Gender Dysphoria Syndrome* (pp. 240-242). Stanford: University of California Press.

Augstein, M. S. (1992). Zur rechtlichen Situation Transsexueller in der Bundesrepublik Deutschland. In F. Pfäfflin & A. Junge (Eds.), *Geschlechtsumwandlung. Abhandlungen zur Transsexualität* (Sex change. Studies on transsexualism) (pp. 103-112). Stuttgart-New York: Schattauer.

Ball, J. (1981). Thirty years experience with transsexualism. *Australian and New Zealand Journal of Psychiatry, 15*, 39-43.

Benjamin, H. (1964 a). Nature and management of transsexualism. With a report on thirty-one operated cases. *Western Journal of Surgery. Obstetrics and Gynecology, 72*, 105-111.

Benjamin, H. (1964 b). Transsexualismus, Wesen und Behandlung (Transsexualism. Its nature and treatment). *Nervenarzt, 35*, 499-500.

Benjamin, H. (1964 c). Clinical aspects of transsexualism in the male and female. *American Journal of Psychotherapy, 18*, 458-469.

Benjamin, H. (1966). *The Transsexual Phenomenon*. New York: Julian Press.

Benjamin, H. (1967). Transvestism and transsexualism in the male and female. *Journal of Sex Research, 3*, 107-127.

Blanchard, R., Steiner, B., & Clemmensen, L. (1985). Gender dysphoria, gender reorientation, and the clinical management of transsexualism. *Journal of Consulting and Clinical Psychology, 53*, 295-304.

Blanchard, R., Legault, S., & Lindsay, W. (1987). vaginoplasty outcome in male-to-female transsexuals. *Journal of Sex and Marital Therapy, 13*, 265-275.

Dudle, U. (1989). *Klinische Follow-Up Studie an operierten Transsexuellen. Eine Beurteilung der Behandlungsresultate von 18 operierten Mann-zu-Frau und 11 Frau-zu-Mann Transsexuellen unter Einbezug des gesamten vorhandenen klinischen Materials über geschlechtsdysphorische Patienten* (Follow-up of transsexuals after sex-reassignment surgery. Evaluation of the outcome of 18 male-to-female and 11 female-to-male transsexuals including all clinical data on gender dysphoric patients). Bern: Medical. Dissertation, Universität Bern.

Edgerton, M., & Meyer, J. (1973). Surgical and psychiatric aspects of transsexualism. In C. Horton (Ed.), *Plastic and reconstructive surgery of the genital area*. Boston: Little, Brown & Co.

Eicher, W. (1983). 95 Fälle von primärer Genital-Transformationsoperation bei Transsexualität (95 cases of primary sex-reassignment surgery in transsexuals). *Mitteilungen der Gesellschaft für praktische Sexualmedizin 3*, 28-33.

Eicher, W. (1984). Transsexualismus (Transsexualism). Stuttgart-New York: Gustav Fischer.

Eicher, W., Schmitt, B., & Bergner, C. M. (1991). Transformationsoperation bei Mann-zu-Frau-Transsexuellen. Darstellung der Methode und Nachuntersuchung von 50 Operierten (Sex-reassignment surgery in male-to-female transsexuals. Surgical procedure and follow-up of 50 patients). *Zeitschrift für Sexualforschung, 4*, 119-132.

Fahrner, E.-M., Kockott, G., & Duran, G. (1987). Die psychosoziale Integration operierter Transsexueller (The psychosocial integration of transsexuals). *Nervenarzt, 58*, 340-348.

Fogh-Anderson, P. (1969). Transsexualism, an attempt at surgical management. *Scandinavian Journal of Plastic and Reconstructive Surgery, 3*, 61-64.

Gandy, P. (1973). Follow-up on 74 gender dysphoric patients treated at Stanford. In D. Laub & P. Gandy (Eds.), *Proceedings of the second interdisciplinary symposium on gender dysphoria syndrome* (pp. 227-229). Stanford: University of California Press.

Green, R., & Fleming, D. (1990). Transsexual surgery follow-up: Status in the 1990s. *Annual Review of Sex Research 1*, 163-174.

Hastings, D. (1974). Postsurgical adjustment of male transsexual patients. *Clinics in Plastic Surgery, 1*, 335-344.

Hastings, D., & Markland, C. (1978). Post-surgical adjustment of twenty-five transsexuals (male-to-female) in the University of Minnesota Study. *Archives of Sexual Behavior, 7,* 327-336.

Herms, V. (1989). Results and follow-up of surgical transformed transsexuals. In W. Eicher (Ed.), *Plastic surgery in the sexually handicapped* (pp. 129-133). Berlin: Springer.

Hertz, J., Tillinger, K., & Westman, A. (1961). Transvestitism. Report on five hormonally and surgically treated cases. *Acta Psychiatrica Scandinavica, 37,* 283-294.

Hoenig, J., Kenna, J., & Youd, A. (1970 a). Social and economic aspects of transsexualism. *British Journal of Psychiatry, 117,* 163-172.

Hoenig, J., Kenna, J., & Youd, A. (1970 b). A follow-up study of transsexualists: Social and economic aspects. *Psychiatrica Clinica, 3,* 85-100.

Hoenig, J., Kenna, J., & Youd, A. (1971). Surgical treatment for transsexualism. *Acta Psychiatrica Scandinavica, 47,* 104-133.

Hore, B., Nicolle, F., & Calnan, J. (1975). Male transsexualism in England. Sixteen cases with surgical intervention. *Archives of Sexual Behavior, 4,* 81-87.

Hunt, D., & Hampson, J. (1980). Follow-up of 17 biological male transsexuals after sex-reassignment surgery. *American Journal of Psychiatry, 137,* 432-438.

Ihlenfeld, C. (1973). Outcome of hormonal-surgical intervention in the transsexual condition: Evaluation and management. In D. Laub & P. Gandy (Eds.), *Proceedings of the second interdisciplinary symposium on gender dysphoria syndrome* (pp. 230-233). Stanford: University of California Press.

Jayaram, B., Stuteville, O., & Bush, I. (1978). Complications and undesirable results of sex-reassignment surgery in male-to-female transsexuals. *Archives of Sexual Behavior, 7,* 337-341.

Jones, H. (1972). The surgical approach to problems of sexual identification. *Medical College of Virginia Quarterly, 8,* 34-36.

Junge, A. (1987). *Behandlungsverlauf und Katamnese von operierten weiblichen Transsexuellen* (Treatment and follow-up of female-to-male transsexuals). Hamburg: PhD-Thesis, Universität Hamburg.

Kando, T. (1973). *Sex change. The achievement of gender identity among feminized transsexuals.* Springfield, Ill.: Charles C Thomas Pbl.

Kernberg, O. F. (1975). *Borderline conditions and pathological narcissism.* New York: Jason Aronson.

Kockott, G., & Fahrner, E.-M. (1988). Male-to-female and female-to-male transsexuals: A comparison. *Archives of Sexual Behavior, 17,* 539-546.

König, M., Cornu, F., Blaser, A., Zingg, E., Stirnemann, H., & Trost, B. (1978). Transsexualismus (Transsexualism). *Schweizer Medizinische Wochenschrift, 108,* 437-444.

Kröhn, W., Bertermann, H., Wand, H., & Wille, R. (1981). Nachuntersuchungen bei operierten Transsexuellen (Follow-up of transsexuals after sex-reassignment surgery). *Nervenarzt, 52,* 26-31.

Kuiper, A. (1985). *Transseksualiteit en Hulpverlening. Een 'ex post facto' onderzoek naar het effect van de geslachtsaanpassende behandeling bij 143 trans-*

seksuellen (Treatment of transsexualism. Follow-up of 143 transsexuals who are in treatment for sex-conversion). Utrecht: Instituut voor Klinische Psychologie en Persoonlijkheidsleer (IKPP) van de Rijksuniversiteit Utrecht (RUU) (Typoskript).

Kuiper, B., & Cohen-Kettenis, P. (1988). Sex reassignment surgery: A study of 141 Dutch transsexuals. *Archives of Sexual Behavior, 17*, 439-457.

Laub, D., & Fisk, N. (1974). A rehabilitation program for gender dysphoria syndrome by surgical sex change. *Plastic & Reconstructive Surgery, 53*, 388-403.

Lindemalm, G., Körlin, D., & Uddenberg, N. (1986). Long-term follow-up of 'sex change' in 13 male-to-female transsexuals. *Archives of Sexual Behavior, 15*, 187-210.

Lothstein, L. (1980). The postsurgical transsexual: Empirical and theoretical considerations. *Archives of Sexual Behavior, 9*, 547-563.

Lundström, B. (1981). *Gender dysphoria. A social-psychiatric follow-up of 31 cases not accepted for sex reassignment*. Hisings Backa: University of Göteborg Press.

Lundström, B., Pauly, I., & Wålinder, J. (1984). Outcome of sex reassignment surgery. *Acta Psychiatrica Scandinavica, 70*, 289-294.

Mate-Kole, C., Freschi, M., & Robin, A. (1990). A controlled study of psychological and social change after surgical gender reassignment in selected male transsexuals. *British Journal of Psychiatry, 157*, 261-64.

McCauley, E., & Ehrhardt, A. (1984). Follow-up of females with gender identity disorders. *Journal of Nervous and Mental Disease, 172*, 353-358.

McEwan, L., Ceber, S., & Dawns, J. (1986). Male-to-female surgical genital reassignment. In W. Walters & M. Ross (Eds.), *Transsexualism and Sex Reassignment* (pp. 103-112). Melbourne: Oxford University Press.

McKee, E. (1976). Transsexualism: A selected review. *Southern Medical Journal, 69*, 185-187.

Meyer, J., & Reter, D. (1979). Sex reassignment. Follow-up. *Archives of General Psychiatry, 36*, 1010-1015.

Money, J. (1971). Prefatory remarks on outcome of sex reassignment in 24 cases of transsexualism. *Archives of Sexual Behavior, 1*, 163-165.

Money, J. (1986). *Lovemaps. Clinical concepts of sexual/erotic health and pathology, paraphilia, and gender transposition in childhood, adolescence, and maturity*. New York: Irvington Pbl.

Money, J., & Brennan, J. (1968). Sexual dimorphism in the psychology of female transsexuals. *Journal of Nervous and Mental Disease, 147*, 487-499.

Money, J., & Ehrhardt, A. (1970). Transsexuelle nach dem Geschlechtswechsel (Transsexuals after sex change). *Beiträge zur Sexualforschung, 49*, 70-87.

Money, J., & Primrose, C. (1968). Sexual dimorphism and dissociation in the psychology of male transsexuals. *Journal of Nervous and Mental Disease, 147*, 472-486.

Pauly, I. (1965). Male psychosocial inversion: Transsexualism. *Archives of General Psychiatry, 13*, 172-181.

Pauly, I. (1968). The current status of the change of sex operation. *Journal of Nervous and Mental Disease, 147*, 460-471.

Pauly, I. (1974 a,b). Female transsexualism: Part I and II. *Archives of Sexual Behavior, 3*, 487-526.

Pauly, I. (1981). Outcome of sex reassignment surgery for transsexuals. *Australian and New Zealand Journal of Psychiatry, 15*, 45-51.

Pfäfflin, F. (1981). Psychiatric and legal implications of the new law for transsexuals in the Federal Republic of Germany. *International Journal of Law & Psychiatry, 4*, 191-198.

Pfäfflin, F., & Junge, A. (1990). Nachuntersuchung von 85 operierten Transsexuellen (Follow-up of 85 transsexuals after sex-reassignment surgery). *Zeitschrift für Sexualforschung, 3*, 331-348.

Pfäfflin, F., & Junge, A. (1992). Nachuntersuchungen nach Geschlechtsumwandlung. Eine kommentierte Literaturübersicht 1961-1991 (Follow-up studies after sex-reassignment surgery. A review 1961-1991). In F. Pfäfflin & A. Junge (Eds.), *Geschlechtsumwandlung. Abhandlungen zur Transsexualität* (Sex change. Studies on transsexualism) (pp. 149-457). Stuttgart-New York: Schattauer.

Pomeroy, W. (1967). A report on the sexual histories of twenty-five transsexuals. *Transactions of the New York Academy of Science, 29*, 444-447.

Randell, J. (1969). Preoperative and postoperative status of male and female transsexuals. In R. Green & J. Money (Eds.), *Transsexuals and Sex Reassignment* (pp. 355-381). Baltimore, Md.: Johns Hopkins Press.

Ross, M., & Need, J. (1989). Effects of adequacy of gender reassignment surgery on psychological adjustment: A follow-up of fourteen male-to-female patients. *Archives of Sexual Behavior, 18*, 145-153.

Sigusch, V., Meyenburg, B., & Reiche, R. (1979). Transsexualität (Transsexualism). In V. Sigusch (Ed.), *Sexualität und Medizin* (Sexuality and medicine) (pp. 249-311). Köln: Kiepenhauer & Witsch.

Simona-Politta, M. L. (1983). *Transsexualismus. Eine evaluative katamnestische Untersuchung von 12 Transsexuellen (5 weiblichen, 7 männlichen) nach Geschlechtsumwandlungsoperation* (Transsexualism. A follow-up of 12 transsexuals [5 females, 7 males] after sex-reassignment surgery). Bern: Medical. Dissertation, Universität Bern.

Sörensen, T. (1981 a). A follow-up study of operated transsexual males. *Acta Psychiatrica Scandinavica, 63*, 486-50.

Sörensen, T. (1981 b). A follow-up study of operated transsexual females. *Acta Psychiatrica Scandinavica, 64*, 50-64.

Spengler, A. (1980). Kompromisse statt Stigma und Unsicherheit. Transsexuelle nach der Operation (Compromises instead of stigma and uncertainty. Transsexuals after surgery). *Sexualmedizin, 9*, 98-103.

Springer, A. (1981). *Pathologie der geschlechtlichen Identität. Transsexualismus und Homosexualität. Theorie, Klinik, Therapie* (Pathology of gender identity. Transsexualism and homosexuality. Theory, clinic, therapy). Wien-New York: Springer.

Stein, M., Tiefer, L., & Melman, A. (1990). Follow-up observations of operated male-to-female transsexuals. *Journal of Urology, 143*, 1188-1192.

Steiner, B. (1976). Vor und nach Geschlechtskorrektur. Langfristige Beobachtung transsexueller Patienten notwendig (Before and after sex-transformation. The need for long-term observation of transsexual patients). *Sexualmedizin, 5,* 842-845.

Stoller, R. (1975). *Perversion. The erotic form of hatred.* New York: Pantheon Books.

Stone, C. (1977). Psychiatric screening for transsexual surgery. *Psychosomatics, 18,* 25-27.

Stürup, G. (1976). Male transsexuals. A long-term follow-up after sex reassignment operations. *Acta Psychiatrica Scandinavica, 53,* 51-63.

Täschner, K., & Wiesbeck, G. (1988). Psychische und soziale Befunde bei Transsexuellen (Psycho-social findings in transsexuals). *Deutsche Medizinische Wochenschrift, 113,* 1154-1157.

Tsoi, W. F., Kok, L. P., & Long, F. Y. (1977). Male transsexualism in Singapore: A description of 56 cases. *British Journal of Psychiatry, 131,* 405-409.

Turner, U., Edlich, R., & Edgerton, M. (1978). Male transsexualism. A review of genital surgical reconstruction. *American Journal of Obstetrics and Gynecology, 132,* 119-132.

Vogt, J. (1968). Five cases of transsexualism in females. *Acta Psychiatrica Scandinavica, 44,* 62-88.

Wålinder, J.(1967). *Transsexualism. A study of forty-three cases.* Göteborg: Akademieförlaget.

Wålinder, J., & Thuwe, I. (1975). *A social-psychiatric follow-up study of 24 sex-reassigned transsexuals.* Göteborg: Akademieförlaget.

Wålinder, J., Lundström, B., & Thuwe, I. (1978). Prognostic factors in the assessment of male transsexuals for sex reassignment. *British Journal of Psychiatry, 132,* 16-20.

Walker, P. A., Berger, J. C., Green, R., Laub, D. R., Peynolds, C. L., & Wollman, L. (1985). Standards of care: The hormonal and surgical sex reassignment of gender dysphoric persons. *Archives of Sexual Behavior, 14,* 79-90.

Walser, P. (1968). Verlauf und Endzustände bei Transvestiten und Transsexuellen (The course and final outcomne of transvestite and transsexual developments). *Schweizer Archiv für Neurologie, Neurochirurgie und Psychiatrie, 101,* 417-433.

Wiegand, G. (1984). *Transsexuelle vor und nach der Operation. Verlaufsstudie an 47 Patienten* (Transsexuals before and after surgery. Follow-up of 47 patients). Heidelberg: Medical. Dissertation, Universität Heidelberg.

Wiesbeck, G., & Täschner, K. (1989). Transsexualität "Grenzsituation des menschlichen Lebens." Postoperative Untersuchungsergebnisse bei Transsexuellen (Transsexualism. 'Extremities of life.' Postoperative evaluations of transsexuals). *Therapiewoche, 39,* 721-725.

Will, M. R. (1992). '. . . ein Leiden mit dem Recht.' Zur Namens-und Geschlechtsänderung bei transsexuellen Menschen in Europa ('. . . the legal problems are a headache.' European legislation as regard change of name and change of sex for transsexuals). In F. Pfäfflin & A. Junge (Eds.), *Geschlecht-sumwandlung. Abhandlungen zur Transsexualität* (Sex change. Studies on transsexualism) (pp. 113-148). Stuttgart-New York: Schattauer.

Wyler, J. (1978). *Transsexualismus* (Transsexualism). Basel: Medical. Dissertation, Universität Basel.

Wyler, J., Battegay, R., Krupp, S., Rist, M., & Rauchfleisch, U. (1979). Der Transsexualismus und dessen Therapie (The treatment of transsexualism). *Schweizer Archiv für Neurologie, Neurochirurgie und Psychiatrie, 124,* 43-58.

Zingg, E., König, M., Cornu, F., Wildholz, A., & Blaser, A. (1980). Transsexualismus: Erfahrungen mit der operativen Korrektur bei männlichen Transsexuellen (Transsexualism: The clinical experience with the surgical treatment of male transsexuals). *Aktuelle Urologie, 11,* 67-77.

Clinical Management
of Gender Dysphoria in Young Boys:
Genital Mutilation
and DSM IV Implications

L.M. Lothstein, PhD, ABPP

SUMMARY. In this study the clinical management of young boys (average age 6) who are gender identity disordered and who present with genital self injurious behavior is discussed. It is argued that the symptom of genital mutilation is often missed because it is not asked for in the clinical interview. A review of the literature, and case history material, suggests that the symptom of genital self injurious behavior is only found among children who are gender dysphoric. Young boys who experience severe gender dysphoria also have a serious affective disorder which must be addressed. In order to address the clinical emergency and to assist the families in getting the necessary treatment for their children specific recommendations for interventions are made.

INTRODUCTION

In this paper the phenomenon and treatment of an extreme form of gender identity disorder in childhood will be presented. Typically, the syndrome of boyhood gender identity disorders presents with a pattern of crossdressing, stereotypical feminine behavior, gender envy towards girls, an avoidance of male behaviors and rough and

L.M. Lothstein is Director of Psychology at The Institute of Living in Hartford, CT. Dr. Lothstein is Associate Professor, Departments of Psychiatry, UCONN Health Center, Farmington, CT, and Case Western University, Cleveland, OH; and Adjunct Professor, University of Hartford, Hartford CT.

tumble play, and an identification with the female role (Greenson, 1966; Esman, 1970; Galenson, Vogel, Blau, & Roiphe, 1985; Meyer & Dupkin, 1985; Green, 1987; Haber, 1991). In addition, a high percentage of these boys present with severe and incapacitating separation anxiety disorder (Coates, Friedman, & Wolfe, 1991). A subgroup of these severely gender impaired boys may also present a unique clinical picture which includes profound depressive symptomology and suicidal or parasuicidal behaviors. These behaviors may be expressed as *genital dysphoria* with the major symptom being a stated desire for *genital mutilation* or *autocastration* (Lothstein, 1988).

While the literature on childhood gender identity disorders makes mention of the phenomenon of *genital dysphoria* it has not been fully integrated into the DSM III-R understanding of the disorder. Indeed, the authors of DSM-III-R are not decisive on the issue of *genital dysphoria*. While they state that "In rare cases a boy with this disorder claims that his penis or testes are disgusting or will disappear, or that it would be better not to have a penis or testes," the issue of genital mutilation or autocastration is avoided.

A recently published interim report from the DSM-IV subcommittee on gender identity disorders (Bradley, Blanchard, Coates, Friedman, & Wolfe, 1991) continues in this tradition by ignoring the possible relationship between *genital dysphoria* and the clinical DSM-III-R diagnosis of Gender Identity Disorder of Childhood. While it may be rare for gender impaired boys to mutilate their genitals, it may also be underreported because of the disgust and terror it instills in the therapists. Subsequently, "accidental" injury to a boy's genitals (secondary to zipper injuries or unexplained blunt trauma) may mask severe gender dysphoria which is being hidden by the child or ignored by the adult (Benians & Goldacre, 1984; Cass, Gleich, & Smith, 1985; Muram, 1986; Young & Feinsilver, 1986). All the adult may see is a confused or depressed child, with or without overt symptomatic presentation of the clinical syndrome of gender identity disorder in childhood. Unless a child is asked about his intent to harm his penis the incidence and prevalence of this symptom may never be known.

The symptom of self injurious behaviors in children (e.g., head banging, eye gauging, skin burning, cutting, etc.) is not rare (Singh,

1981; Pattison & Kahan, 1983; Farazza, 1987; Griffin, Ricketts, Williams et al. 1987; Hyman, Fisher, Mercugliano & Cataldo, 1990) and treatment paradigms are available to treat these self injurious behaviors (Linscheid, Iwata, Ricketts et al. 1990). However, only gender impaired children (or children with atypical depressions who are concealing their gender dysphoria) target their genital for self injurious behaviors. The symptom of genital abuse is not openly discussed and there are no specific treatment paradigms to treat their symptom of genital abuse.

In the adult literature several studies have been published focusing on men who mutilate their genitals or engage in autocastration (Farah & Cerny, 1973; Goldfield & Glick, 1973; Fisch, 1987; Money, 1988; Coleman & Cesnik, 1990). Among adults who do mutilate their genitals or engage in genital amputation, the clinical picture of an underlying gender identity disturbance is the rule. This group includes adults who are transsexuals (Lowy & Kalavakis, 1971; Money & DePriest, 1976; Haberman & Michael, 1979); acutely psychotic adults who are struggling with feminine feelings and homosexual submission to father (Hall, Lawson, & Wilson, 1981); or men with severe gender conflicts who acted out in a dissociated state or while drunk or drugged (Blacker & Wong, 1963; Schneider, Harrison, & Beigel, 1974; Greilsheimer & Groves, 1979). Like their child counterparts, these men are distinguished from other adult men who are self injurious on the basis of their severe gender identity confusion in which the male genital becomes the target of their gender confusion and hatred. In addition, there are some adult males who injure their genitals secondary to blunt trauma related to unusual masturbation practices (Hill, 1980). As a group these men are not recognized as having gender dysphoria.

It is unknown to what extent adults who have *genital dysphoria* also experienced that dysphoria as children. *Genital dysphoria* is documented in mythology (Frazier, 1922), identified cross culturally (Cawte, Djagamara & Barrett, 1966; Nanda, 1984), and found throughout the life cycle across a variety of individuals (men and women, boys and girls) who experience *gender dysphoria*. In an effort to identify those women (Wise, Dietrich, & Segall, 1989) and men who attempt to mutilate their genitals secondary to gender dysphoria the designation *Caenis Syndrome* (Goldney & Simpson,

1975) for women, and *Klingsor Syndrome* (Schweitzer, 1990) for men, has been suggested. More recently Money (1988) and Coleman & Cesnik (1990) have identified, and labeled, a syndrome (Skoptic Syndrome) which involves a disturbance in the body image and accompanying castration and mutilation of the genitals. This syndrome is compared to, and differentiated from, the practice of the Hijras of India who have a desire to be neutered as part of an initiation rite.

It is hoped that this report will sensitize clinicians to the seriousness of *genital dysphoria* in the symptomatic presentation of a subgroup of childhood gender identity disorders in boys and provide a clinical paradigm for responding to the child who presents with this symptom. Essentially, this means recognizing a major affective component in the clinical symptom picture of childhood gender identity disorders (Lothstein, 1980) and not minimizing the self injurious tendencies among these children which may mask a suicidally depressed state (Lothstein, 1988).

Although this paper focuses on boys with *genital dysphoria*, my recent clinical work suggests that a separate paper could be written focusing on the special problems of females who have *genital dysphoria*.

THE MALE CHILD
WITH AUTOCASTRATION WISHES

A review of the literature revealed several studies focusing on gender impaired children who wished to be rid of their penis and testicles (Cohen, 1976; Metcalf & Williams, 1977; Gilpin, Raza & Gilpin, 1979; Bradley, Doering, Zucker et al. 1980; Loeb & Shane, 1982; Lothstein, 1988). While this wish may be expressed verbally it is more likely expressed in play or nonverbally.

Cohen (1976), focusing on a 6 year old gender identity disordered boy in art therapy depicted the child's treatment through his artistic productions. When asked to comment on one of his drawings, the child stated of his penis, "I don't want to look at that thing on me." Metcalf and Williams (1977) reported on the treatment of a 6 year old boy who they identified as "transsexual" who "on a number of occasions asked his parents (if he) could have his penis removed." He expressed a wish to become a woman with a "bosom" and to have a baby. Gilpin, Raza and Gilpin (1979), described a case of "transsexual" symptoms in a 6 year old boy, who was a difficult child with temper tantrums, head banging, and "destruction of everything he could get his hands on." His mother reported sadistic acts including putting a rubber band around a dog's neck (which seemed to be a displacement of his genital mutilation fantasies). Bradley, Doering, Sucker et al. (1980), assessing gender disturbed children, siblings and controls, discovered that among the sample of 15 children (average age 6.9 years), the boys wanted their penis removed, disliked their erections, sat to urinate, and wanted to have babies.

Loeb and Shane (1982) described the case of a 5 year old boy with a transsexual wish who "would hide his penis between his legs, stating he was ashamed of it and would like to cut it off. . . . (he told his mother) how lucky she was that she did not have a 'wiener.' " In an unpublished study, Coates and Person (1985) reported that 45% of 25 gender disturbed boys repudiated their anatomy. Rage tantrums, and suicidal behavior was elicited in response to separation from mother. Coates, Friedman, and Wolfe (1991) stated that in the boy with a gender identity disorder "the penis is the emblem of the gender he is trying to be rid of. At this stage, boys often urinate only by sitting down. They tape their penis between their legs and pretend they have a vagina, and in some cases they talk about wanting to have their penis cut off." In one report (Bloch, 1978) there was a clear parental wish to annihilate their gender impaired children. The children exhibited a defensive transsexual fantasy in order to preserve the self from the parent's murderous wishes. For these children a complete change of self versus a change in genital structure was necessary for survival.

These studies point to the possibility that genital mutilation fantasies (sometimes appearing clinically as the disappearing penis-game by either tucking the penis between the legs or by binding and taping the penis) may not be uncommon among gender disturbed boys. Given the enormous pain, disgust, and anxiety that genital mutilation behavior may stir up in the therapist, many clinicians, hearing a case of genital mutilation, may defensively disengage from that material and focus instead on the surface characteristics of the disorder, that is, the crossdressing and cross gender behavior.

THEORETICAL UNDERPINNINGS
OF CORE INTERVENTIONS

The theoretical underpinnings which guide my clinical interventions with patients who are diagnosed as having a gender identity disorder are rooted in psychodynamic theory; specifically drawn from the literature on ego psychology, object relations theory and self psychology.

About age 2 the child concretely associates the penis with his maleness (cf. Stoller, 1968, 1975; Roiphe & Galenson, 1981). For those male children whose parental self objects are conflicted about his gender status (they wished for a girl, are disappointed in his "maleness," are threatened by his aggression and anger that surfaced during toilet training, project their own sexual anxieties, and incestuous and bisexual fantasies onto the child) the child may come to view his penis as a dangerous and threatening organ. The penis as a concrete symbol for the male self has been discussed by Limentani (1979) as a precursor of adult transsexual cognitive distortions.

All the parents in this study verbally and nonverbally communicated their genital dysphoria to their son. Why this particular boy was chosen reflects a specific family dynamic. The boys' attempt to hide their penis, to make it go away, or hurt it, was a direct response to their parents' wishes that it go away. In effect, they were sacrificing their penis in order to be loved. The boys experienced their parents as telling them that their penis was offensive, bad, evil and that they were unlovable. When erect these boys became panicked that they would be abandoned for being "bad," that is, having bad thoughts. Their initial attempt to have the parents show pride in their accomplishment (an erect penis) was transformed into terror and anxiety. Given the cognitive capacity of these children (all between 4-6 years of age) their solution was to employ magical thinking and concrete logic expressed as the idea that "the parents won't love me until I get rid of the dreaded penis." In this way the gender dysphoric male child relates his experience of the penis as disgusting, dangerous, violent and wild.

For the gender dysphoric child tumescence is viewed as a lethal act, concretely representing the bad, destructive, evil self. When the penis became erect, "everyone" can see their "bad" sexual thoughts. In this sense, their erections are evidence of their inability to contain the sexual and aggressive urges within the self. Consequently, there can be no secrets and no development of a separate male identity unless those thoughts can be contained within the self. The erect penis, when revealed to the dysfunctional parents, is viewed by them as a dreaded force that must be subdued. In the child's psyche this is equivalent to saying that the male self must "go away," disappear, or be dead. In the child's concrete logic this translates into "I must hurt or remove my penis for my parents to love me."

The theoretical underpinnings which guide the clinical interventions to alleviate the child's *genital dysphoria* were drawn from the findings of *Self Psychology* (Kohut, 1977; Kohut & Wolfe, 1977). In this theoretical framework a separate line of narcissistic development focusing on the development of self esteem and control over the body, is posited. From the perspective of Self Psychology the child's initial experience is that there is no differentiation between the parental self-objects which exert a control over him and his own inner experience of control. Through development the child develops *self regulation* in which the control his self-objects previously had over him is now experienced as his own ability to control his body. He now assumes the control his self-objects previously had over him. In this context the findings of Tolpin (1971) and others support the idea that the development of a cohesive self and the capacity for self-care (Khantzian and Mack, (1983)) are direct results of "the parent's nurturing and protective functions (which are) incorporated into the child's ego capacities in the service of maintaining adequate self-esteem, ego defense mechanisms, and adaptation to reality."

During the phallic stage (around age 3) boys exhibit their erect penis to the parental self-objects for confirmation, reassurance, and pride. The integration of the genital schema into the body schema is only accomplished when the child's self-object milieu provides the appropriate mirroring of his genital exhibitionism. Mirroring is a term used by self psychology to describe a developmental phase of child development in which the mothering object provides support for, and encouragement of, the child's grandiosity and the child's attempts at "active mastery of the world." This is a crucial developmental task of body narcissism which helps the child consolidate the image of his penis and testicles into his genital body schema (Socarides, 1988) and establishes it as an integral part of his body image. Parents who are shocked by the child's genital displays and who fail to soothe the child's anxiety and confusion about his erect penis (which they may associate with forbidden thoughts about sexuality and aggression) leave the child feeling guilty, shameful, and frightened of his genitals. Rather than having his penile exhibitionism converted into pride and self esteem (around his newly discovered body part through self-object mirroring, that is not treating the mother as separate but as supporting of, and reflecting his body self), the boy experiences a deflation in self esteem, and a need to split off his penis from his body image. The very organ which was associated with the boy's developing maleness, and which was dreaded by the parents, now becomes viewed as something to be rid of. One mother who placed her 5 year old in a warm tub to "make it (his erection) go away" indelibly communicated to her son that she despised his penis (that is, his maleness) and wished it (his maleness) to go away.

Kohut (1977) argued that empathic failure by the child's self-objects during the mirroring and idealizing phase of development can lead to impaired narcissistic development, low self esteem, and a tendency towards self fragmentation and self pathology. Failures "in empathy and traumatic disappointments in idealized parental figures" were regarded as "central determinants in narcissistic disturbances" which were hypothesized to lead to self pathology, perverse sexuality, and hatred of the body.

In one of their case histories Khantzian and Mack (1983) concluded that: "the capacity for self care grows in the context of a loving parent's communications that he or she values the child and therefore considers the child worth taking care of. The child incorporates this message and comes to value himself enough to protect himself from injury." A child who perceives himself as being unloved and unresponded to may develop excessive aggression which "brings about ego disorganization, which in turn causes the individual to become less able to exercise judgment, control, synthesis, reality testing, and related functions that otherwise assure adequate self-care and protection." All of the ideas presented above help to explain why some gender impaired children experience *genital dysphoria* and try to harm their genitals.

ASSESSMENT AND TREATMENT

All the children I evaluated had not yet carried out their plans to mutilate their genitals. Having shared their plans with their parents they were brought for psychological consultation.

The following vignettes underscore the dimension and severity of *gender* and *genital dysphoria* which the children presented.

1. Elliot (age 5) said that "When my penis goes up I get mad and angry. I hate it when it goes up. I want to shoot it off with a gun. I want to get rid of it. I want to shoot myself and die." Once he tried to cut off his penis but was thwarted. His mother also intercepted his attempt to get his father's gun in order to shoot his penis.
2. Robert (age 4) believed that he had a vagina. When his penis became erect he would "pull back his testicles . . . (and) bending his penis" would threaten to cut off his penis with a knife. Robert told his mother: "I want it to come off, it's ugly, I don't like it."
3. Brian (age 4) would beat his erect penis every morning. He told his parents that he hated his penis and wanted to make it go away. He was frightened and angry by his erections. It was only with detumescence that his anxiety lessened and he lost interest in harming his genitals.
4. Doug, (age 4) became so confused when he had an erection that he wished he could be a girl. His confusion was acted out in attempts to remove his penis by putting it between his legs and hitting it.
5. Stanley (age 5) tucked his penis between his legs, identified with female superheros, and hit his penis when erect, trying to make it go away. While in the tub he tried to cut off his penis but was intercepted by mother.

None of the parents contacted their pediatricians. When they sought out mental health consultation their requests were put off. In all cases, these decisions related to the reason for the evaluation (that is, their children were acting like girls and threatening to harm their penis). In some cases the parents may have downplayed the urgency for a consultation because of the "embarrassment" and pain it stirred up in them. When it was discussed, it appeared as if the clinicians were also avoiding the pain. In all cases the health care provider contacted (always a child clinician) asked if I would see the child. In all cases, very experienced child clinicians deferred to me (an expert in gender identity disorders but not an expert in child therapy) and reserved their better judgement to treat the child themselves. The reason for the delay in making the referral may have related to several factors, including, feelings of inadequacy among the child therapists who rarely encountered cases of "transsexual" children (as they called them). To what extent the clinician's own anxiety, fear, disgust, and terror about the child's *genital dysphoric* symptom contributed to the decision not to treat, can only be speculated on.

In most cases these were child experts who had demonstrated a high tolerance for managing self injurious behaviors in non-gender disordered children; self-injurious behaviors which were often severe, and chronic (e.g., headbanging, eye-gouging, body cutting or burning, etc.). Clearly, genital mutilation is a specific kind of self injurious behavior which may have a specific psychodynamic precursor and explanation and arouses a unique set of countertransference, and real, responses in the treating therapist. It is not surprising then, that clinicians, who were familiar with other types of self injurious behaviors and their treatments, might find themselves at a loss to explain, no less treat, a behavior (such as genital mutilation or autocastration) which were so novel and anxiety provoking.

The initial evaluation of these children must include a differential diagnosis to rule out an organic disorder, profound psychopathology (including psychosis) or, child sexual abuse. It is incorrect to assume that child sexual abuse is the rule for every case (including covert sexual abuse). Of the five cases I treated, there was one documented case of sexual abuse and suspected abuse in two others. There was no evidence of sexual abuse in two cases (which does not mean, however, that it did not occur). In one adult case cited in the literature (De Young, 1982) a young woman who mutilated her genitals explained her actions as a direct result of her own childhood sexual abuse. She associated her genitals with her vulnerability to sexual abuse and believed she would be protected in the future if she got rid of her genitals. She was also experiencing considerable shame for the pleasure associated with her assault.

Enough time must be set aside to do an intensive and complete family evaluation (in a short period of time) in order to prevent genital self injurious behavior from occurring. Inpatient psychiatric hospitalization should be considered when the family environment is insufficiently supportive to aid in the child's recovery. In all of my cases no medications or inpatient psychiatric hospitalization was necessary to stabilize the child.

In all five cases, the mothers and children were unable to separate from each other. It was only through progressive stages that the child (and the mother) was able to tolerate being alone in the room with me. In all cases, the children were quite candid with me (in response to direct questioning) of the plan they had to mutilate or amputate their genitals. In addition to having a plan for self injurious behavior (a parasuicidal plan), all of the children experienced depressive symptomology marked by eating disturbances, sleep disorders, phobias, and suicidal feelings. None of them evidenced a tearful depression. Depressive equivalents, in terms of somatization and acting out, were the rule. Their enactments masked their loneliness, isolation, despair, and sadness.

Examples of acting out behavior included the following. One child tried to harm himself in my office by banging into furniture and climbing on cabinets and jumping off. He tried to kill himself by climbing onto, and jumping off, high elevations. He also ran into traffic and had to be restrained. Another child who was emotionally "fused" with his mother, identified with her self-injurious behavior (she was a borderline woman who cut herself), and was virtually ignored when he talked about cutting off his penis. He was also accident prone. Another child was a compulsive eater. He ate to enliven his inner self and avoid profound depressive feelings. While watching television he would cross dress and yearn for contact with the t.v. personalities. However, whenever there was a food commercial he would sit up excitedly, ignore his female garments, become disinterested in female feelings, and savor the food products. He would then stuff himself with any food available. No purging was evidenced. Another child brought a back pack filled with food for the 45 minutes of play therapy. He ate constantly and was aggressive. For him, eating did not alleviate his intense separation anxiety and abandonment depression. He was also suicidal, exhibitionistic, and hyperactive.

All of the children were candid about their hatred, and fear of their penis (especially when erect) and their wish to remove it from their bodies. Focusing on this wish allowed the emergence of material related to their envy of, and wish to be, a girl. All of the children wore girls' clothing, makeup and jewelry, avoided playing with boys, identified as females, sat to urinate, and enacted stereotypical feminine behavior during the initial evaluation and throughout the early to middle phase of therapy. In all instances, this was supported actively, or ignored, by the mothers. It was actively discouraged by the fathers (sometimes through corporal punishment), and brought to their parents' attention by school authorities who viewed the boys' effeminate behavior with concern. All of the boys were isolated from peers because of their fragility, avoidance of rough and tumble play, and their stereotyped female behaviors. They were all viewed as "sissies" by their fathers. One boy who sat to urinate was quite exhibitionistic. He was unmercifully teased by the other boys. This did not lead to compensatory behavior. While he hated the teasing, he would not change his behavior since standing to urinate aroused too much anxiety and aggression.

Initial interventions with the child focused on the following:

1. allowing the child to ventilate his wishes for genital mutilation outside the context of the family but in the presence of his mother so that she could hear his pain for the first time. The mother was instructed to listen and not interrupt the child's play or conversation. The father could also be present but none wished to attend the first session;

2. reframing the child's plan for genital mutilation to view it as covering his feelings of inadequacy, sadness, loneliness, low self esteem and his chronic depression;

3. identifying the child's real pain in the family setting; focusing

on his feminine wishes as depressive equivalents around his dissatisfaction with his maleness and his concerns that as a male his parents would not love him;

4. identifying what else the child would like to change in his life and how he went about fulfilling his needs in the family;

5. talking openly about sexual differences, exploring his ideas of what makes boys and girls different (with a specific emphasis on where babies come from); understanding his anxieties about childbirth (in this context, material on the differences between the sexes is discussed);

6. avoiding pressuring the child to change his behavioral cross-dressing but helping the child to understand how it calms and soothes him, and makes him feel less depressed: allowing him to feel that he is understood and accepted by the therapist irrespective of his cross gender behavior; and

7. finally, the therapist must talk openly about the boy's penis and explore with him how he feels about it and how he experiences his parents' reaction to his penis. Is he proud of it? Are they proud of it? An open discussion about the penis, erections, and the normalcy of erections (what they are, how boys generally react to their erections and how to cope with his genital anxiety, and how confused some boys become about their penis regarding the mistaken association they make between sexual and aggressive feelings and their erections). An open discussion about childbirth must be initiated. Opportunity to discuss sibling issues, the birth of a new sibling and the special meaning a girl baby may have, and the child's feelings about that must be explored. Once the child's depression is broached the therapist must bring up the sadness which accompanies the realization that he cannot become both sexes (cf. Fast, 1984) and that he cannot become pregnant. This news, while setting limits to the boy's grandiosity and implying a depressive position is also greeted with relief. Typically the boys focus on the pain of childbirth and relief that they do not have to go through that.

Conveying an understanding of the child's dilemma in an empathic way removes the child's sense of urgency for genitally mutilative behavior. In this sense therapists must give themselves permission to talk openly about sexual issues with the children. They must also obtain permission from the parents to talk about sexual issues with their children. One therapist, treating a gender dysphoric child, confided that he was unwilling to talk about sex with the child since he thought his colleagues would view this tactic as sexually abusive. If the child is to be successfully treated this countertransference dilemma must be worked through early in the evaluation process.

Meeting with the parents separately is crucial. The therapist must be confident that the child's urgent symptom to harm his genitals will dissipate and be resolved. The therapist must redirect the agenda from the boy's pain to the families' problems. No guilt or accusations should be accepted as an explanation of the families' difficulties. The child's gender problems need to be reframed as part of a larger family issue (e.g., an intergenerational conflict over aggression which is unresolved, a covert bisexual conflict in one or both parents, control issues, etc.). In this context, the child's problems also need to be reframed as relating to conflicts over aggression, gender identity confusion and depression.

In all cases the children exerted enormous control over their parents who feared them and disengaged from them. All of the clinical interventions are done to alleviate the parent's anxiety and guilt so that they can begin to focus on the family problems and not just on the child's symptom. Once this is achieved the child's genital mutilation symptoms disappear.

The parents are informed about specific issues in child development around their son's confusions and anxieties about his penis and erections and the need for him to accept his penis. In this context a mini-lecture is given to the parents. My experience is that both parents are confused about their own genital functioning. Inevitably the father begins talking about his genital insecurities and inadequacies. Once father talks about his early childhood experiences of genital insecurity he is able to identify with his child's suffering as similar to his own unresolved pain. In this way an empathic link is established between the father and his son around their shared genital anxiety. Once the father understands how his parents failed to mirror his genital development he can empathize with his son's pain. Rather than attacking his son for failing to develop an appropriate masculine self image the father can identify with his son's efforts to become a man (which parallel the father's efforts). In this context, the therapy is directed to helping the father understand the nature of his conflicts with his father and any male siblings. Issues of competition, power, and dominance in those relationships must be explored. That is, what was absent in their relationships with father? What did their brothers have that they yearned for? What was his explanation of why he was so anxious, distraught, angry, or symptomatic as a child? Two of the fathers in this study confessed that they were bedwetters. All of the fathers were passive–dependent, with reaction formations to their passivity, angry, and all experienced separation anxiety as children. During this phase of treatment the mother is learning about the difficulty her son, and husband, have in achieving maleness.

The next phase of treatment focuses on instructing the parents (especially father, since it is he who must communicate directly with his son) that it is important to take pride in their son's penis and accept it as part of his body. This means having the parents (through the medium of the father) to go out of their way to say something complimentary about their son's body and specifically his penis as the occasion calls for it. What this does is to give permission to the father to talk to his child about a central configuration in the father-son relationship which is being avoided, that is the difficulties growing up male and achieving masculinity and specifically integrating the penis into a healthy body schema. It also gives permission to the mother, and the family as a whole, to talk about things that are not being talked about.

The mother's inability to separate from her son and allow him to individuate also needs to be addressed. In this context the mother's relationship to her own mother must be broached. All of the 5 mothers in this study had impaired relationships with their own mothers. Their mothers were described as intrusive, depressed, dissatisfied in their marriages, angry and jealous of men, and ambivalent towards their daughters. Each of the mothers felt inadequate as women, were high achievers, successful in their careers, and "wore the pants" in their marriages. They all felt cheated and badgered their husbands; making them the targets of their dissatisfaction and disappointment. Their sexual lives were impoverished and characterized by neediness, unfulfilled desires, disappointment, and a lack of intimacy. In an effort to fulfill their intimacy needs these women turned to their sons for gratification and invited them to join in a secretive liaison with them; confiding in them like friends; treating them as special and unique, and empowering them with having a gift to soothe mother. In all cases the boys were told they were special and different from other men who the mother characterized as aggressive, lacking a nurturant capacity, and rough.

In each case when the child's effeminate nature emerged the parents were consciously disappointed in their son's behavior since they longed for a "real man" to rescue them. In effect, the child's gender identity confusions and inner self structures were moulded by the parents in an effort to control their son's body and mind and prohibit him from ever separating and individuating from mother and revealing of father's deficiencies as a caregiver, an intimate person, and a male. While they jointly collaborated (unconsciously, for the most part) to feminize their son they were disappointed with the final product.

CONCLUSION

Most of the clinical work described above can be accomplished within a two to three week period. The clinician must set aside blocks of time to manage the initial crisis. It has been my experience that this can be accomplished on an intensive outpatient basis without resorting to medication and/or inpatient psychiatric hospitalization. Once the acute phase is passed and the child is no longer talking about injuring his genitals an alliance has been formed for treatment and the child and his parents should enter into a longer term of treatment. I concur with Coates' (1990) recommendation of twice weekly therapy for the child and once a week parent guidance. When this is not possible once a week therapy should be initiated along with parent guidance. Unless the parents are involved in the treatment they are likely to sabotage their son's treatment. In addition, it is important to keep them informed of their son's treatment. Some gender impaired boys also need to be in group therapy in order to develop appropriate social skills (Green & Fuller, 1973).

Once a week therapy with the child is the minimum expectation.

Therapy should be expected to last anywhere from 6 months to three years. Some therapists might argue that family therapy is the treatment of choice for these disorders. Certainly family intervention is critical and regular family meetings are essential. Therapy needs to focus on helping the child develop the appropriate self structures for healthy narcissistic development. Therapy with these children should not be based on biases regarding their future gender identity or sexual orientation. What is critical is that these boys be provided the necessary self structures with which to negotiate the complex realities they have yet to experience.

It is hoped that the ideas in this paper may not only serve as hypothesis generating for future clinical and research in gender identity disorders but may also be used in future revisions of the DSM IV subcommittee working on Gender Identity Disorders, to include reference to the phenomenon of *genital dysphoria* in the new diagnostic nomenclature.

REFERENCES

Benians, R., & Goldacre, P. (1984). Non-accidental injury in children: two cases of concealment of self injury. *British Medical Journal, 289,* 1583-1584.

Blacker, K., & Wong, N. (1963). Four cases of autocastration. *Archives of General Psychiatry,* 169-176.

Bloch, D. (1978). *So The Witch Won't Eat Me: Fantasy and the Child's Fear of Infanticide.* Boston: Houghton Mifflin Company.

Bradley, S., Blanchard, R., Coates, S. et al. (1991). Interim report of the DSM-IV subcommittee on gender identity disorders. *Archives of Sexual Behavior, 4,* 333-343.

Bradley, S., Doering, R., Zucker, K., Finegan, J., & Gonda, G. (1980). Assessment of the gender/disturbed child: A comparison to sibling and psychiatric controls. In J. Sampson (Ed.), *Childhood and Sexuality.* (pp. 554-568). Montreal: Editions Etudes Vivantes.

Cass, A., Gleich, P., & Smith, S. (1985). Male genital injuries from external trauma. *British Journal of Urology, 57,* 467-470.

Cawte, J., Djagamara, N., & Barrett, M. (1966). The meaning of subincision of the urethra to Australian Aborigines. *British Journal of Medical Psychology, 39,* 245-253.

Coates, S. (1990). Personal Communication.

Coates, S., Friedman, R., & Wolfe, S. (1991). The etiology of boyhood gender identity disorder: A model for integrating temperament, development, and psychodynamics. *Psychoanalytic Dialogues,* I, 481-523.

Coates, S. & Person, E. (1985). Extreme boyhood femininity: Isolated findings or pervasive disorder? *Journal of the American Academy of Child Psychiatry*, 24, 702-709.

Cohen, F. (1976). Art psychotherapy: The treatment of choice for a six year old boy with a transsexual syndrome. *Art Psychotherapy*, 3, 55-67.

Coleman, E., & Cesnik, J. (1990). Skoptic Syndrome: The treatment of an obsessional gender dysphoria with lithium carbonate and psychotherapy. *American Journal of Psychotherapy*, 54, 204-217.

De Young, M. (1982). Self-injurious behavior in incest victims: A research note. *Child Welfare*, 61, 577-584.

Esman, A. (1970). Transsexual identification in a three-year old twin–a brief communication. *Psychosocial Process*, 1, 77-79.

Farah, R., & Cerny, J. (1973). Penis tourniquet syndrome and penile amputation. *Urology*, 2, 310-311.

Farazza, A. (1987). *Bodies Under Siege: Self-Mutilation in Culture and Psychiatry*. Baltimore: Johns Hopkins Press.

Fast, I. (1984). *Gender Identity: A Differentiation Model*. New Jersey: Lawrence Erlbaum Associates.

Fisch, R. (1987). Genital self-mutilation in males: Psychodynamic anatomy of a psychosis. *American Journal of Psychotherapy*, 41, 453-458.

Frazier. J. (1922). *The Golden Bough: A Study in Magic and Religion*. London: Macmillan.

Galenson, E., Vogel, S., Blau, S., & Roiphe, H. (1985). Disturbance in sexual identity beginning at 18 months of age. *International Review of Psychoanalysis*, 2, 389-397.

Gilpin, D., Raza, S., & Gilpin, D. (1979). Transsexual symptoms in a male child treated by a female therapist. *American Journal of Psychotherapy*, 33, 453-462.

Goldfield, M., & Glick, I. (1973). Self mutilation of the genitalia. *Medical Aspects of Human Sexuality*. April 219, 236.

Goldney, R., & Simpson, I. (1975). Female genital self-mutilation, dysorexia, and the hysterical personality: the Caenis syndrome. *Canadian Psychiatric Association Journal*, 20, 435-441.

Green, R. (1987). *The "Sissy Boy Syndrome" and the Development of Homosexuality*. New Haven: Yale University Press.

Green, R., & Fuller, M. (1973). Group therapy with feminine boys and their parents. *International Journal of Group Psychotherapy*, 23, 54-68.

Greenson, R. (1966). A transvestite boy and a hypothesis. *International Journal of Psycho-Analysis*, 47, 396-403.

Greilsheimer, H., & Groves, J. (1979). Male genital self-mutilation. *Archives of General Psychiatry*, 36, 441-446.

Griffin, J., Ricketts, R., Williams, D. et al. (1987). A community survey of self-injurious behavior among developmentally disabled children and adolescents. *Hospital and Community Psychiatry*, 38, 959-963.

Haber, C. (1991). Gender identity disorder in a four year old boy. *Journal of the American Psychoanalytical Association,* 39, 107-139.

Haberman, M., & Michael, R. (1979). Autocastration in transsexualism. *American Journal of Psychiatry,* 136, 347-348.

Hall, D., Lawson, B., & Wilson, L. (1981). Command hallucinations and self-amputation of the penis and hand during a first psychotic break. *Journal of Clinical Psychiatry,* 42, 322-324.

Hill, J. (1980). Penile injuries from vacuum cleaners. *British Medical Journal,* 281, 519.

Hyman, S., Fisher, W., Mercugliano, M., & Cataldo, M. (1990). Children with self-injurious behavior. *Pediatrics,* Supplement, 437-441.

Khantzian, E., & Mack, J. (1983). Self preservation and the care of the self. *Psychoanalytic Study of the Child,* 38, 209-232.

Kohut, H. (1977). *The Restoration of the Self.* New York: International Universities Press.

Kohut, H., & Wolf, E. (1977). The disorders of the self and their treatment. *International Journal of Psychoanalysis,* 59, 413-425.

Limentani, A. (1979). The significance of transsexualism in relation to some basic psychoanalytic concepts. *International Review of Psycho-Analysis* 6, 139-153.

Linscheid, T., Iwata, B., Ricketts, R. et al. (1990). Clinical evaluation of the self-injurious behavior inhibiting system (SIBIS). *Journal of Applied Behavioral Analysis,* 23, 53-78.

Loeb, L., & Shane, M. (1982). The resolution of a transsexual wish in a five year old boy. *Journal of the American Psychoanalytical Association,* 10, 419-434.

Lothstein, L. (1980). The adolescent gender dysphoric patient: an approach to treatment and management. *Journal of Pediatric Psychology,* 5, 93-109.

Lothstein, L. (1988). Selfobject failure and gender identity. In A. Goldberg, (Ed.) *Frontiers in Self Psychology: Progress in Self Psychology.* (pp. 213-235). New York: The Analytic Press.

Lowy, F., & Kolivakis, T. (1971). Autocastration by a male transsexual. *Canadian Psychiatric Association Journal,* 16, 399-405.

Metcalf, S., & Williams, W. (1977). A case of male childhood transsexualism and its management. *Australian and New Zealand Journal of Psychiatry,* 11, 53-59.

Meyer, J., & Dupkin, C. (1985). Gender disturbance in children. *Bulletin of the Menninger Clinic,* 49, 236-269.

Money, J. (1988). The Skoptic Syndrome: Castration and genital self-mutilation as an example of sexual body-image pathology. *Journal of Psychology & Human Sexuality,* 1, 113-128.

Money, J., & DePriest, M. (1976). Three cases of genital self-surgery and their relationship to transsexualism. *Journal of Sex Research,* 12, 283-294.

Muram, D. (1986). Genital tract injuries in the prepubertal child. *Pediatric Annals,* 15, 616-620.

Nanda, S. (1984). The Hijras of India: A preliminary report. *Medicine Law,* 3, 59-75.

Pattison, M., & Kahan, J. (1983). The deliberate self-harm syndrome. *American Journal of Psychiatry*, 140, 867-872.

Roiphe, H., & Galenson, E. (1981). *Infantile Origins of Sexual Identity*. New York: International Universities Press.

Schneider, S., Harrison, S., & Beigel, B. (1974). Self castration by a man with cyclic changes in sexuality. *Psychosomatic Medicine*, 2753-70.

Schweitzer, I. (1990). Genital self-amputation and the Klingsor syndrome. *Australian and New Zealand Journal of Psychiatry*, 24, 566-569.

Singh, N. (1981). Current trends in the treatment of self-injurious behavior. *Advances in Pediatrics*, 28, 377-440.

Socarides, C. (1988). *The Preoedipal Origin and Psychoanalytic Therapy of Sexual Perversions*. Connecticut: International Universities Press.

Stoller, R. (1968). *Sex and Gender*, New York: Science House.

Stoller, R. (1975). *Sex and Gender: Vol. II: The Transsexual Experiment*. New York: Jason Aronson.

Tolpin, M. (1971). On the beginnings of a cohesive self. Psychoanalytic Study of the Child, 26, 316-352.

Wise, T., Dietrich, A., & Segall, E. (1989). Female genital self mutilation: Case reports and literature review. *Journal of Sex and Marital Therapy*, 15, 269-274.

Young, L., & Feinsilver, D. (1986). Male genital self-mutilation: Combined surgical and psychiatric care. *Psychosomatics*, 27, 513-517.

Female Gender Disorder:
A New Model and Clinical Applications

Jeremy Baumbach, PhD
Louisa A. Turner, PhD

SUMMARY. A broad model of female gender disorder is presented
in which distinctions are drawn between gender dysphoria, defined
as an internal emotional state of discontent or discomfort associated
with one's gender, the fantasized solution of wishing to be the other
sex, and the request for hormonal and/or surgical sex reassignment.
This model is applied to three clinical cases, representing both transsexual and non-transsexual types of gender disorder. Subsequent discussion explores some of the questions raised by considering these
components separately, and also presents some hypotheses about the
nature of gender dysphoria in women.

Persons with gender disorders present many challenges to the
clinician, the first of which is diagnosis. DSM-III-R, the American
Psychiatric Association's most recent version of the Diagnostic and

Jeremy Baumbach and Louisa A. Turner are affiliated with the Center for
Human Sexuality at Case Western Reserve University School of Medicine. Requests for reprints should be directed to Jeremy Baumbach, who is currently at
Yukon Family Services Association, 210 Elliott Street, Whitehorse, Yukon, Canada, Y1A 2A2.

The theoretical component of this paper was developed as part of the first
author's doctoral dissertation, undertaken at the University of Saskatchewan with
financial support from the Social Sciences and Humanities Research Council of
Canada in the form of a Doctoral Fellowship. A previous version of this paper,
entitled "Variations of gender dysphoria in females" and co-authored by Terry
Tobias, PhD, was presented at the Eleventh International Symposium on Gender
Dysphoria sponsored by the Harry Benjamin International Gender Dysphoria
Association, in Cleveland, OH, October, 1989. The authors would like to acknowledge Terry Tobias for her valuable contributions to the earlier draft and for
her editorial assistance in the preparation of this version.

Statistical Manual of Mental Disorders (1987), provides clear criteria for the diagnosis of Transsexualism, a severe gender disorder. For transsexualism to be diagnosed, a person must have reached puberty and must experience (a) a persistent discomfort and sense of inappropriateness about his/her assigned sex, and (b) a persistent preoccupation for at least two years with getting rid of his/her primary and secondary sex characteristics and acquiring the sex characteristics of the other sex. These criteria facilitate accurate diagnosis of transsexualism. Having made such a diagnosis, the clinician can access a substantial literature which will assist in both the conceptualization of the patient and the selection of a suitable treatment approach.

DSM-III-R criteria for the diagnosis of Gender Identity Disorder of Adolescence or Adulthood, Nontranssexual Type (GIDAANT) are equally clear. For GIDAANT to be diagnosed, a person must have reached puberty and must experience (a) a persistent or recurrent discomfort and sense of inappropriateness about his/her assigned sex, (b) persistent or recurrent cross-dressing in the role of the other sex, either in fantasy or actuality, but not for the purpose of sexual excitement (as in Transvestitic Fetishism), and (c) no persistent preoccupation (for at least two years) with getting rid of his/her primary and secondary sex characteristics and acquiring the sex characteristics of the other sex (as in Transsexualism). These criteria facilitate accurate diagnosis of GIDAANT; however, having made such a diagnosis, the clinician will find much less in the literature to assist in the understanding, conceptualization, and treatment of persons diagnosed with this less extreme gender disorder. This is especially true in the case of biological females. Persons with gender disorders who meet the criteria for neither transsexualism nor GIDAANT may warrant a diagnosis of Gender Identity Disorder Not Otherwise Specified (GIDNOS). Such persons are by no means rare, and may indeed often present requesting psychotherapy, but the literature pertaining to them is even more sparse. In sum, especially in the case of the biological female, if a diagnosis of transsexualism cannot be made, the clinician is left with little guidance as to the understanding, conceptualization, and treatment of the patient.

It is the purpose of this paper to present a simple model of gender disorders in biological females; whether it is also applicable to biological males is undetermined at present. While it does not generate specific diagnoses, this model provides a way to conceptualize both transsexual and non-transsexual types of gender disorder, and thus may improve understanding and facilitate treatment planning. In the following pages, the model will be first explicated and then applied to clinical cases, with discussion to follow.

THE MODEL

This model proposes that the classic transsexual presentation results from the combination of three components:

1. A problem: Gender dysphoria
2. A fantasized solution: The wish to be the other sex
3. An action: The request for hormonal and/or surgical sex reassignment

In the person who meets the DSM-III-R diagnostic criteria for transsexualism and who presents at a gender clinic pursuing sex reassignment, each of these three components is present. In such a case, they co-exist, but these components are potentially separate and independent. It is our contention that persons manifesting less severe gender disorders can be conceptualized as having one or two, but not all three, of these components. Before elaborating on this hypothesis, each component of the model will be explored in more detail.

Gender Dysphoria: The Problem

Although the term "gender dysphoria" was coined more than fifteen years ago (Fisk, 1973), there remain some differences regarding its specific definition. Some authors (e.g., Lothstein, 1979) have considered the belief that one is, or the wish to be, the other sex and the request for sex reassignment to be core features of gender dysphoria, while others (e.g., Blanchard, 1990a) have understood gender dysphoria as potentially existing in the absence of a request for sex reassignment. In our model, the features of gender dysphoria, the wish to be the other sex, and the request for sex reassignment are construed as separate, albeit related, phenomena. Given that dysphoria is a feeling of discontent or discomfort, we would define gender dysphoria as a feeling of discontent or discomfort associated with one's gender. As such, gender dysphoria speaks neither to gender identity nor to cross-gender identification, and it does not encompass any treatment-seeking behavior. Rather, it is defined simply as an internal emotional state of discontent or discomfort associated with one's gender.

This definition of gender dysphoria focuses attention on the affect associated with being male or female, rather than on cognitive or behavioral aspects. The role of affect vis-a-vis gender has not been adequately explored (Fagot & Leinbach, 1985), but recently there have been some pointers in its direction. First, from the clinical arena, are Zucker and Green's (1989) comments in a chapter on the treatment of gender disordered children. These authors distinguish between cognitive and affective features, and report that, while some young children actually do misclassify their gender, more commonly there is correct self-labeling as a boy or girl but discontent with this assignment and persistent desire to be of the other sex. It is this affective aspect which is seen to require therapeutic attention. Second, some empirical support for the central role of affect comes from a study by Rozee-Koker, Dansby and Wallston (1985). These authors were attempting to identify a cross-racial role-transcendent female identity. Using a factor analytic approach, they explored the hypothesized cognitive, behavioral and affective components. To their surprise, the cognitive and behavioral components were not represented in the factor-analytic solution, but the affective response to being a woman was found to be a highly reliable unidimensional factor. From these data at least, the authors concluded that positive feelings about being a woman are the primary ingredient in a strong female identity.

In sum, gender dysphoria is defined here as a subjective internal affective state of discomfort or discontent associated with one's gender. These feelings may give rise to a great variety of cognitions and behaviors.

The Wish to Be the Other Sex: The Fantasized Solution

The wish to be the other sex has been reported in a variety of clinical and nonclinical populations of women other than those diagnosed as transsexual and requesting sex reassignment. David Lynn (1959) reported that "as high as 31% of adult females recall consciously having been aware of the desire to be of the opposite sex" (p. 132); Benjamin (1966) stated that "in our culture about twelve times more women would like to have been born men than vice versa" (p. 179); and both Stoller (1979) and Meyer (1982) have described the mothers of gender dysphoric persons as wishing to be male. While these data suggest that the wish to be the other sex may be relatively common in women, they do not speak to the stability, persistence, or motivations for the wish. Specifically, one cannot ascertain from these data whether, as our model requires, the wish serves as a fantasized solution.

In a recent study of a nonclinical sample of young women who had wished to have been born a boy (Baumbach, 1987), the wish did appear to always serve as a fantasized solution to some problem. However, qualitative analysis of subjects' responses also revealed that many of the underlying problems were not related to gender dysphoria (e.g., wishing to be male in order to attain some male prerogatives, or because she perceived that she would then be able to escape from some difficulty or threat). In these cases, the wish served as a fantasized solution to a problem, but the problem was not one of gender dysphoria. Similarly, in the clinical literature it has been noted quite often that homophobia rather than gender dysphoria may underlie a woman's wish to be male; that is, a lesbian may find her homosexuality so intolerable that she wishes to be male, for then her erotic attractions to women would be heterosexual (Kirkpatrick & Friedmann, 1976; Lothstein, 1983; Shtasel, 1979). Here the wish to be the other sex is the fantasized solution to a problematic sexual orientation.

While it cannot be presumed to exist simply on the basis of the wish's existence, gender dysphoria may well be the problem that the wishful fantasy solves. It is certainly not surprising that this would be the case. In our culture, there are males and females, and that is all (Kessler & McKenna, 1978). If a person experiences discontent and discomfort as one sex, it makes some sense to entertain the wish to be the other. The consequences of experiencing both gender dysphoria and the wish to be the other sex (the first two components of our model) will vary according to the individual. Some of the possible outcomes will be explored later in this paper.

The Request for Sex Reassignment: The Action

It is the treatment-seeking behavior of requesting sex reassignment that most often brings the gender disordered individual into contact with the health professional.[1] Consequently, the vast majority of clinical and research data is drawn from the study of these persons, potentially biasing our perspective and artificially constricting our grasp of the breadth of gender disorders. One goal of this paper is to spur interest in the study of those persons struggling with some degree of gender disturbance, but not requesting sex reassignment. Some cases exemplifying this population are presented in the next section.

The gender disordered individual's request for sex reassignment reflects this culture's construction of gender as physical. In our culture, genitals are the essential sign of gender: A female is a person with a vagina, and a male is a person with a penis (Kessler & McKenna, 1978). Thus, if there is any way to become a member of the other sex, it must include the acquisition of appropriate genitals and, to a lesser extent, the acquisition of other physical characteristics. As Pauly and Edgerton (1986) wrote, "In an ironic sense, transsexualism may be considered iatrogenic, in that advances in surgical technique now permit the realization of fantasies of sexual metamorphosis" (p. 318).

While our cultural litmus test for gender is physical (genital), there are many other actions persons can and do take in accordance with their fantasized solution long before requesting sex reassignment. The combination of gender dysphoria and the wish to be the other sex typically results in a degree of identification with the other sex, and, to the extent that this is acted upon, the manifestation of social sex-role characteristics associated with the other sex. As a person exhibits more social sex-role characteristics of the other sex, one would expect both others' reactions and self-perception to reflect this reality. Over time, such a person may come to see him or herself as "different" from others of the same biological sex, and indeed there would be some truth to this perception. Here then, is the feeling that one is or should be the other sex that is so often reported by transsexuals. In such cases, the request for sex reassignment is the last action, but certainly not the only action, taken in pursuit of their fantasized solution. In other cases, little or no action is taken prior to the request for sex reassignment.[2]

CLINICAL APPLICATIONS

The cases described in this section will highlight the range of gender disorder in females. The first case is a woman with all three components of the model, the classic "transsexual" patient who comes to clinical attention at a gender identity program. The second case presents a woman who came to a sexuality clinic for therapy and has only the first two components of the model, that is, an internal experience of gender dysphoria and a childhood wish to be a boy. In the third case, another woman who sought treatment at a sexuality clinic, only the gender dysphoria component of the model is present

Gender Dysphoria, the Wish to Be Male, and the Request for Sex Reassignment: The Transsexual

This is a case of a woman with lifelong gender dysphoria who has opted to live as a man, take male hormones, and undergo mastectomy, hysterectomy, and phalloplasty. When she first came to our clinic, Linda was a 30-year old Caucasian biological female presenting in a unisex fashion wearing jeans, sneakers, and sweatshirt, sporting a short androgynous hairstyle, and exhibiting masculine demeanor and gestures. Known at the time to her work colleagues and her few friends as Linda, she reported a longstanding discomfort with her female status and a growing feeling that she could not get on with her life until she made the transition to living as a male.

Linda gave the following history. She was the first of two daughters born to older parents. Her younger sister, nicknamed Sissy, was perceived by the family as very feminine from birth and as "totally different from Linda." Linda was known rather for her energy and activity level, and the family stories surrounding her babyhood seemed to cast her primarily in the role of nuisance as a result of these temperamental qualities. Linda's father worked on the night shift, and was, for unknown reasons, Linda's primary caretaker, even though Linda's mother did not work outside the family home. Linda has few pleasant memories of her mother, currently describing her as "quick to accuse, hot-tempered, stubborn, and hard to get along with." She always felt closer to her father, whom she characterizes as "a big and quiet man who is easy to get along with." Her most pleasant childhood memories are of accompanying her father on errands to the grocery store, or better yet, the barber shop. Linda also had a significant relationship with her grandmother, whom she remembers as kind, giving, and gentle, and "as totally different from [her] mother."

Linda's gender dysphoria and wish to be a boy date back to around kindergarten. She recalls a marked preference for rough and tumble play, a wish for boys rather than girls as playmates, and an aversion to dolls. She resented the fact that she and her sister were constantly referred to as "the girls," as she had a strong early sense that she and her sister did not belong in the same category and that she did not want to be identified as a girl. She hated wearing dresses, and got into daily struggles with her mother about them, usually losing. She was able, despite her mother's disapproval and wishes otherwise, to wear her hair in a short haircut. When she was seven, she met a male friend of her parents whose name was Len, probably short for Leonard. She begged to shorten her name to Lin, and pronounce it Len, but her family refused. Linda believes that she became a kind of loner, burying herself in books about male heroes and imagining herself in their place. She also describes herself as becoming "a stubborn, independent, and bull-headed person," hanging on to her secret wish to be a boy. She never spoke of her wish to be a boy, and believes her parents saw her as a tomboy and thought it was a phase that would pass.

Due to her father's work, the family moved about three times a year until Linda was 12 years old. With changing schools so frequently, she was often either ahead of the other students in her studies and bored, or behind them and struggling. In addition to feeling "out of sync" academically with the other kids in her class, Linda found it difficult to repeatedly make new friends, only to leave them after several months. Linda's mother did not make any active efforts to help the kids become integrated into their new life beyond locating and dropping them off at the local recreation center. As Linda was a talented athlete, sports activity was the main way she could make friends, as "they always wanted [her] on their team." Indeed, because of her prowess, Linda was usually able to organize coed sports and teams, which she preferred because she really wanted to play with boys.

When Linda was ten years old, her grandmother died. Linda describes this as "the first major trauma in [her] life." At the age of twelve, Linda's father changed jobs and started to be away from home for months at a time. Linda felt abandoned by him, angry and sad. Linda's mother went to work full-time, leaving the two girls to fend for themselves after school. Linda recalls this, the beginning of her adolescence, as a very lonely time. Linda characterizes puberty as "the second major trauma in [her] life." Developing breasts and having menstrual periods were horribly disappointing to Linda, confirming that she was biologically female and shattering her longheld secret belief that at puberty she would finally develop into a male.

Linda began experiencing sexual feelings at about the age of 13, and from the beginning her attractions were exclusively to female partners. Linda says that this did not surprise her greatly, but that it further confirmed for her that she "was really different from other girls and really more like boys." Linda "went to the library," spending long hours seeking out information about her alternatives, and became aware of the phenomenon of transsexualism at about this time. Learning of the possibility of gender transition was a tremendous relief for her; as she put it, "I finally found a place where I belonged." This further strengthened her wish to be a male and her resolve that this was the right course for her.

During and shortly after college, Linda had two important sexual relationships with women. These consisted primarily of Linda stimulating her partner to orgasm, without allowing her partner to see or touch her own breasts or genitals. Both of these women identified themselves as heterosexual, and both left Linda and went on to date men. Linda also never masturbated, as touching herself genitally brought her too close to intolerable feelings about her femaleness. She has never had an orgasm of which she is aware.

After college, Linda concentrated on establishing herself in her work as a research engineer. She remained active in many coed sports, playing in golf, volleyball, and softball leagues. She continued to contemplate a transsexual lifestyle, but felt daunted by the difficulties of making the gender transition at her very good job. She also believed that her family would never accept her as a male, and she repeatedly delayed her plans to tell them of her wishes.

Despite these perceived obstacles, Linda decided to proceed with sex reassignment. She began to go out in the evenings to local bars dressed as a man and wearing a mustache. Next she arranged independently for a physician to give her testosterone injections, and within about three months applied for and got a new job in a new city as a man. Although Linda passed well as male, and legally changed her name to Larry, she continued to be a loner because of her fear that she would be recognized as a biological female. Larry has gone on to have bilateral mastectomies, hysterectomy, and phalloplasty through an established gender clinic program. He is currently married to a woman who thinks of him as a biological male who has undergone surgical repair of his genitals due to some unspecified trauma.

Larry speaks eloquently about the costs of his transsexual adaptation. Larry is estranged from his family, having been rejected by his parents. He feels sad about his inability to father children. He believes that he will always feel somewhat different from other men, and that he will never be at ease, for instance, in a locker room. Most of all, he experiences a sense of personal discontinuity, which includes feeling unable to speak openly about his history and sensing that no one knows him completely, and being constantly concerned that someone from his past will recognize him in his new identity.

For the purposes of comparing and contrasting our model with that presented in DSM-III-R, we provide our DSM-III-R diagnosis of Linda/Larry:

    Axis I: 302.50 Transsexualism
    Axis II: No diagnosis

Gender Dysphoria and the Wish to Be Male

This is a case of a young woman who has had longstanding gender dysphoria and the childhood wish to be a boy, but who never considered living as a man or pursuing sex reassignment. Pat is an attractive, highly-functional 23-year old single Caucasian woman who works in a maternity shop while going to college part-time. Her facial features and carriage are somewhat masculine, but her stylish dresses and make-up lend her an overall feminine appearance.

Pat came to therapy saying "I don't know who I am sexually. I'm worried that I am a lesbian." When asked what caused this worry, Pat described a longstanding discomfort about herself that she characterized as "a feeling of not being totally female." This discomfort is at its most intense when she is with a group of heterosexual female friends and she feels very different from them, in her words, like "the odd man out." The only time in her life that she has not felt this way around women was a time in college when she lived in a dormitory with a group of self-identified gay women. These women were athletic like she was, wearing sweatclothes and seen as "jocks" by others. In this group, she felt comfortable, similar, and like she belonged, even though she is quite clear that she has sexual attractions only to men and never to women. One of the initial processes of therapy was to clarify for her the difference between gender identity and sexual orientation.

After some time, Pat let go of the fear of being lesbian and framed her difficulties as "about being female." Then she began to speak of other aspects of her gender dysphoria. Her menstrual periods had always been infrequent and irregular. This made her feel "not feminine," and made her worry about defectiveness as a woman. Though she had always wanted to have children, she wondered about her physical capacity to do so. She spoke at length about her struggles with her appearance, of how she had not worn blue jeans in five years in an attempt to look more feminine. She wanted to wear dresses and look pretty, but she was afraid to look sexy, and she often felt she could not tell the difference. She also wished that she did not know so much about sports. A more feminine woman, she thought, would watch a football game with her boyfriend and, with an uncomprehending look, ask him "What's a first down?" Finally, Pat saw her ambitions in business (she intended to own a chain of maternity stores one day), as masculine, and thus had difficulty integrating them into her self-image as a woman.

Pat felt that her discomfort about femaleness made it very hard for her to be close to other people. With women friends, she felt overwhelmed by a sense of differentness and inadequacy that made it quite difficult for her to share herself. She also considered her gender dysphoria to be a major factor in what she called her "failure at heterosexual relationships." She had had several relationships of some length, and at the age of 20 had been engaged to marry one young man. Pat broke their engagement for reasons which she is not able to articulate clearly even now. Since that time, she has dated, but gets frightened and withdraws when the relationship becomes emotionally and/or sexually intimate. She notes, however, that her gender dysphoric feelings are at their least troublesome when a man is initially interested in a relationship with her, but then quickly return when the liaison becomes sexual. She describes herself as a "sexual moron," and her characterizations of her sexual activities, vague and poorly articulated, demonstrate her sexual naivete and discomfort.

Pat was the first-born child of middle-class Catholic parents. During her early childhood, Pat was closer to her father than to her mother. Pat's mother was quite feminine in her appearance, but was also perceived by Pat as unattuned, unempathic, and cold. In explanation of her difficulties in her relationship with her mother, Pat says "She was always wanting me to be just like her and I didn't want to do it." In contrast, Pat's father, a warm, expressive man, was very involved with Pat. As he worked the afternoon shift at his job, he was often home during the day and seemed to function as Pat's primary parent, taking Pat with him on his daily errands and tasks. Pat's most cherished memories of early childhood are of accompanying her father to hardware stores and lumberyards. Pat and her father would play ball together, and he praised and enjoyed her natural athletic ability.

By the age of about four, Pat had developed into a tomboy, preferring jeans to dresses, boys to girls as playmates, and sports and cowboy games to dolls. She was very proud that she had a unisex name, and felt good when someone would mistake her for a boy. She tried to master the art of standing up to urinate. She felt more like a boy than a girl, did not like the fact that she was a girl, and did not like girls. She recalls wishing that she were a boy or could become a boy, but she does not remember voicing this to anyone. She believes that the intensity of her wish was not overwhelming because she was acting like a boy, with the only cost being her mother's disapproval. She felt protected from the brunt of her mother's disappointment by the closeness with and attention from her father. She felt very different from her sister, Sally, two years younger. Sally was always closer to their mother than their father, and early developed into a frilly, feminine girl.

When Pat was four years old, her brother, Tim, was born. As Pat puts it, "That's when everything changed." Her father was delighted to finally have a son, and Pat felt replaced. As the baby moved into toddlerhood, Pat's father began to take Tim, instead of Pat, everywhere with him. He no longer seemed interested in playing catch with Pat, and began to encourage her to become more feminine and spend more time with her mother. Pat felt abandoned and bereft, and turned reluctantly back to her mother, where she met anger, envy, lack of sympathy, and demands for compliance and femininity. Pat's mother did not support Pat's athletic ability, and refused to comfort her when she hurt herself while engaging in rough play. Pat oppositionally clung to this vestige of her relationship with her father in her participation in school sports, until she injured her back during a sports event in high school and had to give up athletics for good. Pat's mother insisted that she dress more femininely, and she felt forced to comply. A relationship pattern began to develop that is still in place at the present time, in which Pat's mother wishes Pat to be feminine, unassertive, and to have tastes and opinions which mirror her own. She continues to be angry and envious whenever Pat's life plan differs from what she has had in mind for Pat.

Pat's feeling that she was more like a boy and her wish to be a boy gradually began to fade. As she puts it, "It was futile. I saw now that what my father had wanted was a boy, not me as I was. I knew I couldn't really be a boy, and I knew I couldn't get him back. But I also couldn't feel very good about myself." Thus it was that Pat was left with the gender dysphoria that brought her into treatment. Pat's sense of differentness from other women continues, and her feminine identification remains tenuous and full of feelings of inadequacy.

Pat's treatment centered around dispelling her idea that she was a lesbian and understanding the roots of her gender dysphoria, thus allowing her to feel more comfortable as a woman. It was also necessary to work through some separation issues with her mother in order to permit Pat to develop her own ideas about what kind of woman she wanted to be. Fortunately, she was also able to develop a rapprochement with her father, this time based on a closeness in which she could be feminine. She has developed stronger friendships with women. There is still much work to be done on exploring and integrating her sexuality and having more satisfying relationships with men.

Using DSM-III-R criteria, Pat's diagnosis would be:

Axis I: 302.91 Sexual Disorder Not Otherwise Specified
         (Feelings of inadequacy about her femininity)
Axis II: None

Gender Dysphoria Only

This case involves a young woman who has had lifelong gender dysphoria but who never had a wish either presently or historically to be a male. Susan is a pretty though rather asexual 25-year old Caucasian woman who is married to a kind, passive man and has a young son. She has completed two years of college and is a part-time office worker. Her demeanor is intelligent, straightforward, and sincere.

Susan initially came into therapy with her husband to work on their marital problems. Within several months, the focus shifted to Susan's longstanding sense that there was something wrong with her, though she did not know what. Her self-esteem was very low, she said, and sometimes she had periods of hating herself. Several months of individual therapy clarified that these enigmatic negative feelings were specifically about her gender, and she summed these feelings up in the simple phrases "I hate being a woman" and "I hate myself as a woman." Susan did not think that being a man or being more masculine presented an answer; indeed, she never entertained any other solution to this problem other than working in therapy toward feeling better about being a woman. She longed for a comfortable female identity, speaking wistfully of her inability to be pretty, her clumsiness with make-up and hair styling, her ignorance of fashion, and her perceived incompetence at such stereotypically feminine activities as sewing and cooking.

Susan's self-hatred as a woman was enacted in several arenas. First, her sexuality was dominated by masochistic sexual fantasies in which she could reach orgasm only by imagining herself being hurt or humiliated by a "father-like figure." Her sexual behavior with her husband was entirely conventional, but she had very little desire for sex with him and often did not become aroused.

A similar theme was repeated in Susan's avocation of writing. Susan had long been a fan of romance novels, and had aspired to write her own. During therapy, Susan wrote a book, except that it turned out to be more pornographic than romantic. She remarked upon her inability to write about love and the ease with which graphic details of scenes like rape came to her.

Susan also felt that an affair that she had had with a man at work had something to do with her hatred of herself as a woman. This man, whom she described as masculine and charismatic, had bedded many women at their workplace. He repeatedly seduced Susan in a semi-coercive manner, had sex with her with little care about her comfort or enjoyment, and then ignored or demeaned her for weeks afterward. Susan felt "addicted" to him, and had tremendous difficulty saying no to sex with him. Their affair finally ended only when he left town.

Lastly, Susan was extremely relieved that her child was a son. She felt that she would be unable to take care of a daughter, and that she would feel impelled to physically abuse her. At one point, Susan purchased a female dog, to whom she gave a name that she had picked out to give a daughter. Within several months, she was hitting and kicking the animal, and then felt enraged by the dog's subsequent submissiveness, which she described as a "typical female way to be."

Susan's family history provides some explanation of the developmental roots of her gender dysphoria. Susan's father was a normally passive, ineffectual man who nevertheless frequently exploded in anger and became physically abusive to his wife and children. Susan characterized him as making up for an inner lack of self-esteem with boastful, dominating outward behavior. Susan's mother was a self-focused, needy, histrionic woman who was unable to protect her children from the outbursts of their father, and seemed to enjoy vicariously his power over them.

These parents shared a conscious ideal of women as feminine, pretty, delicate, helpless, and unassertive creatures. This view was apparent in such opinions as that women were too refined to be good politicians and in this Catholic family's religious over-preoccupation with the Virgin Mary. Coexisting, however, was a more unconscious and devaluing view of women as cowardly, sexually objectified, and victimized. This was apparent in a number of examples such as the following: Susan's parents entered her home one day to encounter Susan's dog, who promptly roiled over on her back to have her stomach scratched. Susan's father laughed, saying, "You sure can tell that dog is female. The minute a man walks into the room, she's on her back." This complicated view of femaleness then was the family context into which Susan was born.

Susan's conception, occurring three months into her parents' marriage, was unplanned and was not greeted with enthusiasm. The pregnancy was a difficult one. Susan was not considered to be a "pretty" baby, and, plagued by colic, her disposition was not thought of as placid or sweet or, most importantly, feminine. In contrast, Susan's sister, younger by a year and nicknamed "Princess" by the father, was a lovely, docile baby who rarely cried and was more cuddly. (Susan's sister went on to become an unassertive homemaker whose femininity is praised in the family but who is also dominated and physically abused by her husband.)

Susan recalls very early feelings of hating being a girl in her family. She did not feel like a pretty child, and remembers her mother always being frustrated with the outcome when she attempted to dress Susan up in a feminine manner. She was repeatedly and unfavorably compared with her pretty, feminine sister by both parents. Furthermore, Susan was smart and she could do things well, which was also viewed as rather unfeminine in her family and therefore mildly discouraged. The only good thing Susan could think of about being female was that her brother received more severe abuse from her father than did she and her sister.

Susan, however, was not really a tomboy either. She tried unsuccessfully to be athletic as a child; she attempted to join team sports and school track meets but suffered severe asthma attacks with physical exertion. When she wore pants, she was sometimes mistaken for a boy, as she was taller and lankier than most girls her age; however, she experienced these errors as humiliating indications of her failure to be feminine.

If she could not feel love and acceptance from her parents as a girl, Susan's solution, she believes, was to try to be what she called a "good girl." To be so, she became an excessively obedient, compliant, inoffensive child, and she minimized her competencies, especially her intelligence. At a less conscious level, she was probably also trying to escape from her devalued role. Susan retrospectively feels that her solution failed, that she could not be "good enough" to feel recognized and valued in her family, but her efforts show that there may be any number of solutions to the problem of gender dysphoria other than the wish to be male, in this instance, conformity and obedience.

Why did Susan not entertain a wish to be a boy? The answer may lie in the fact that two common routes to a masculine identification in young girls were either not available or offered nothing positive to Susan. First, she did not have skill in stereotypically masculine activities, like sports, and therefore was thwarted in her attempts to be a "jock" or tomboy. Second, she did not have in her father a loved and valued adult male figure with whom to identify. In fact, for as long as she could remember, Susan had viewed her father with fear and disgust, as "an emotionally sick man" who poorly contained his aggression and sexuality. Without natural abilities in the athletic realm and without a positive male role model, Susan may have been left with little basis upon which to form a wish to be male. Shut out from the role of valued female, unable to find recognition as a "good girl," and with little reason to look to being a boy, Susan was stuck with herself as, in her words, a "poor excuse for a girl."

The major goals in therapy for Susan were to improve her self-esteem as a woman and relieve her depression The transference played a central role in this process, as the therapist was often seen as a comfortably feminine but competent woman. Susan began to like herself more as a woman, at least sometimes. She became more feminine in her appearance, experimenting with dresses, makeup, and hair permanents. She prided herself on several successful embroidery projects. She reentered college and was doing well. Perhaps most importantly, she decided to try for another child and felt comfortable and even excited about the possibility of having a daughter.

Using DSM-III-R criteria, Susan's diagnosis would most likely be:

> Axis I: 300.40 Dysthymic disorder
>   302.79 Sexual aversion disorder
>   302.83 Sexual masochism (mild)
>   302.91 Sexual disorder not otherwise specified
>   (Marked feelings of inadequacy concerning femininity)
> Axis II: 301.83 Borderline traits

DISCUSSION

DSM-III-R diagnoses of Linda/Larry, Pat, and Susan highlight their important differences; however, DSM-III-R limitations also obscure their similarities, for while their responses to it are strikingly different, these women share an underlying gender dysphoria. The model proposed allows us to better conceptualize them and women like them, and to begin to talk about at least some of their struggles as importantly related to gender dysphoria. As illustrated in these cases, such a formulation has significant treatment implications. It also provokes many questions, whose exploration has the potential to enrich understanding and conceptualization of gender disorders. We will briefly explore some of these below.

Why Do Only Certain Gender Dysphoric Women Who Wish to Be Male Request Sex Reassignment?

We would suggest that three of the influential factors in this regard are (a) the inability/unwillingness to continue coping with the gender dysphoria in whatever way they have previously, (b) the willingness to tackle the reality of sex reassignment, and (c) the severity of the gender dysphoria. Most often, persons seek sex reassignment only after a number of other coping options, undertaken more or less purposefully, have failed. Often there have been attempts to conform, attempts to fit into the gay community, attempts to avoid it all by withdrawal or self-distraction, and so on. Then something happens that leads the person to reach out for sex reassignment–perhaps, as in Linda/Larry's case, there is a feeling that she cannot get on with her life as a female, or perhaps something happens to free her up, or conversely, to make a previously tolerable niche less so. In any event, a point of reckoning is reached and passed. Then, the person must be willing to tackle the reality of sex reassignment, which may be quite discrepant from her fantasy of being male, and in addition poses many practical hurdles. In our modern society, there are many complexities to changing gender roles, there are significant potential costs to such a change (e.g., loss of employment, occupation, residence, family, friends, physical normalcy, procreative potential, etc.), and there are limitations to sex reassignment, especially vis-à-vis genital surgery for biological females. These and various other individual considerations will influence whether, in reality, sex reassignment is perceived as an acceptable and viable solution to the gender dysphoria. We would also suggest that the outcome of this process is greatly influenced by the severity of the gender dysphoria. Indeed Dickey and Steiner (1990) have commented that "less intensely gender-dysphoric patients often self-select against sex reassignment when confronted with the various hurdles involved" (p. 139). Of course, several additional questions are prompted by these thoughts: What do we actually mean by intensity or severity of gender dysphoria? And what are its relevant dimensions or components? More on these questions later.

Why Do Only Certain Gender Dysphoric Women Develop the Wish to Be Male?

Our model proposes that the gender dysphoric woman's wish to be male rests on her perception of this as a solution for her gender dysphoria. In order to function as a solution, it must both address the problem and offer something better. The women who wish to be male seem to feel uninterested/inept in the girl's or woman's role *and* better suited to the boy's or man's role; as Linda/Larry put it, "really different from other girls and really more like boys." Both Linda/Larry and Pat described feeling different from women, highlighted by the contrast with their own feminine sisters, and felt themselves to be like boys in their interests, activity levels, athletic abilities, and in Linda/Larry's case, sexuality. (What effect does emerging adolescent sexuality have on an individual's struggles with gender dysphoria? Were Pat to have found herself attracted to females, would her outcome have been different, and, if so, how?) In contrast, Susan, while "a poor excuse for a girl" and different from her feminine sister, seems to have had no sense of herself as better suited to being male. Furthermore, Linda/Larry's and Pat's early bonds with their fathers seem to have contributed to a positive conception of maleness, while for Susan this was absent. Consequently, for Linda/Larry and Pat, being male could be construed as an attractive resolution to their gender dysphoria, while Susan was left without this out. Another possibility is that the development (or lack thereof) of the wish to be the other sex results from a qualitative difference in the gender dysphoria. If this is the case, what is the nature of this difference?

Why Do Only Certain Gender Dysphoric Women Persist in Their Wish to Be Male?

Research with a nonclinical sample of women indicated that the wish to be the other sex was relinquished either when the problem prompting that fantasized solution itself remitted or when the woman accepted that the wish was, for various reasons, not a real solution (Baumbach, 1987). No comparable research has been conducted with gender dysphoric women, however, it seems likely that those who persist in their wish to be male both continue to believe that being male would resolve their gender dysphoria and are somehow able to avoid an awareness that this cannot really happen (e.g., Pat's "I knew I couldn't really be a boy") except, as they later find, in the guise of sex reassignment. Are some gender dysphoric women compelled to persist with their wish to be male because of the severity of their gender dysphoria? Or do they lack the ego development to cope differently with their gender dysphoria, perhaps being generally prone to using fantasy as a defense? Are some gender dysphoric women better equipped to pursue their dreams, being, like Linda/ Larry, "stubborn, independent and bull-headed"? In this understudied area there are currently no answers, only questions.

What Is the Nature of Gender Dysphoria?

Earlier we defined gender dysphoria as an internal affective state of discomfort or discontent associated with one's gender. We would now hypothesize that gender dysphoria arises from the inability to integrate femaleness into a positive sense of self. We would expect "solutions" to this integration problem to vary along a continuum. In the cases presented in this paper, we have at one extreme Linda/ Larry, who sacrifices her femaleness but retains a positive sense of self, and at the other, Susan, who maintains a sense of herself as a woman, but hates herself and is dysfunctional as such, with Pat somewhere between the two. We suggest that these women share not only their gender dysphoria, but that in all three cases it rests on their inability to integrate femaleness into a positive sense of self.

There seems to be another important dimension along which gender dysphoric women vary. From an external perspective, it could be described as the degree to which the gender dysphoria is overlaid by masculine strivings, or the breadth and depth of cross-gender behavior (unlike some other authors, for example, Blanchard (1990b), we would not consider this dimension to be the continuum of gender dysphoria itself); however, the women themselves usually talk about this as "feeling different from other women." We hypothesize then, that the second dimension along which gender dysphoric women vary is their sense of self as different ("different in kind") from other women. In the cases presented, the sense of differentness is very strong in Linda/Larry, moderate in Pat, and minimal (if present) in Susan. As exemplified by our cases, the feeling of differentness from women is often associated with wishes to be male, but it may persist long after the wish has been given up.

We construe this paper as a beginning, not an end. We wish our hypotheses to be understood as discussion points, not final formulations. We believe that there is some value to distinguishing between the internal emotional problem of gender dysphoria, the fantasized solution of wishing to be the other sex, and the action of requesting sex reassignment. Separating these components allows us to explore each from a different perspective than previously and to explore their interactions, as we began to do in this paper. It also spurs new questions and ideas; for instance, perhaps learning negative meanings for femaleness (Susan) or very constricted definitions (Pat) or coming to associate it with threat and unlovableness result in gender dysphoria, while innate temperamental characteristics and early positive identifications with the father result in masculine strivings (the wish to be the other sex). Separating these components also orients us to study a greater range of persons with gender disorders. Perhaps the treatment of those with less severe gender dysphoria has something to teach us about helping those with severe gender dysphoria. At the very least, we hope that the model we have presented will provide clinicians with an alternative way to conceptualize and think productively about those patients with gender disorders who slip between the cracks of current diagnostic classification systems.

NOTES

1. Previously it was noted that gender dysphoria cannot be presumed to underlie the wish to be the other sex. Similarly, the request for sex reassignment should not be assumed to be motivated by gender dysphoria.

2. It is worth noting that some individuals cross-live without sex reassignment or treatment seeking; however, it is unknown whether these persons have gender dysphoria and/or the wish to be male.

REFERENCES

American Psychiatric Association (1987). *Diagnostic and Statistical manual of mental disorders* (3rd ed. rev.). Washington, D.C.: Author.

Baumbach, J. (1987). *Beyond gender identity.* Unpublished doctoral dissertation, University of Saskatchewan, Saskatoon, Canada.

Benjamin, H. (1966). *The transsexual phenomenon.* New York: Warner Books.

Blanchard, R. (1990a). Gender identity disorders in adult men. In R. Blanchard and B.W. Steiner (Eds.), *Clinical management of gender identity disorders in children and adults* (pp. 49-76). Washington, D.C.: American Psychiatric Press.

Blanchard, R. (1990b). Gender identity disorders in adult women. In R. Blanchard and B.W. Steiner (Eds.), *Clinical management of gender identity disorders in children and adults* (pp. 79-91). Washington, D.C.: American Psychiatric Press.

Dickey, R., & Steiner, B.W. (1990). Hormone treatment and surgery. In R. Blanchard and B.W. Steiner (Eds.), *Clinical management of gender identity disorders in children and adults* (pp. 139-158). Washington, D.C.: American Psychiatric Press.

Fagot, B.I., & Leinbach, M.D. (1985). Gender identity: Some thoughts on an old concept. *Journal of the American Academy of Child Psychiatry, 24,* 684-688.

Fisk, N. (1973). Gender dysphoria syndrome (the how, what, and why of a disease). In D. Laub and P. Gandy (Eds.), *Proceedings of the Second Interdisciplinary Symposium on Gender Dysphoria Syndrome* (pp. 7-14). Palo Alto, CA: Stanford University Press.

Kessler, S.J., & McKenna, W. (1978). *Gender: An ethnomethodological approach.* New York: John Wiley & Sons.

Kirkpatrick, M., & Friedmann, C.T.H. (1976). Treatment of requests for sex-change surgery with psychotherapy. *American Journal of Psychiatry, 133,* 1194-1196.

Lothstein, L.M. (1979). Psychodynamics and sociodynamics of gender-dysphoric states. *American Journal of Psychotherapy, 33,* 214-238.

Lothstein, L.M. (1983). *Female-to-male transsexualism: Historical, clinical and theoretical issues.* Boston: Routledge & Kegan Paul.

Lynn, D.B. (1959). A note on sex differences in the development of masculine and feminine identification. *Psychological Review, 66,* 126-135.

Meyer, J.K. (1982). The theory of gender identity disorders. *Journal of the American Psychoanalytic Association, 30,* 381-418.

Pauly, I.B., & Edgerton, M.T. (1986). The gender identity movement: A growing surgical-psychiatric liaison. *Archives of Sexual Behavior, 15,* 315-329.

Rozee-Koker, P., Dansby, P.G., & Wallston, B.S. (1985). In search of a cross-racial female identity: The quest for commonality. *Academic Psychology Bulletin, 7,* 269-286.

Shtasel, T.F. (1979). Behavioral treatment of transsexualism: A case report. *Journal of Sex and Marital Therapy, 5,* 362-367.

Stoller, R.J. (1979). Fathers of transsexual children. *Journal of the American Psychoanalytic Association, 27,* 837-866.

Zucker, K.J., & Green, R. (1989). Gender identity disorder of childhood. In *Treatments of Psychiatric Disorders: A Task Force Report of the American Psychiatric Association* (Vol. 1, pp. 661-670). Washington, D.C.: American Psychiatric Association.

A Comprehensive Approach
to the Treatment of Gender Dysphoria

Walter O. Bockting, Drs
Eli Coleman, PhD

SUMMARY. After a brief historical review of the clinical management of gender dysphoria, the authors argue for a comprehensive treatment model that recognizes a wide spectrum of gender identity disorders. This treatment model explores the meaning of a gender dysphoric individual's desire for sex reassignment in the context of the individual's biography and psychosociosexual adjustment. Unlike previous treatment approaches, this model makes no attempt to identify the 'true' transsexual. The model's treatment tasks are: assessment, management of comorbid psychiatric disorders, facilitation of identity formation, sexual identity management, and aftercare. The implications of this treatment model for classification and ethical standards of care are discussed.

HISTORICAL CONTEXT

A review of the history of treatment approaches to gender dysphoria and transsexualism reveals a series of shifts in conceptualization that have had dramatic implications for clinicians and their gender dysphoric clients. Before the widely publicized surgical sex reassignment of Christine Jorgenson in 1953 (Hamburger, Sturup &

Walter O. Bockting is Instructor and Coordinator of the Gender Dysphoria Program at the Program in Human Sexuality, and Eli Coleman is Associate Professor and Director of the Program in Human Sexuality, Department of Family Practice & Community Health, Medical School, University of Minnesota.

Correspondence should be addressed to Walter O. Bockting, Drs, Program in Human Sexuality, 1300 South 2nd Street, Suite 180, Minneapolis, MN 55454.

Dahl-Iversen, 1953) and publication of Harry Benjamin's classic work *The Transsexual Phenomenon* (1966), restrictive conceptualizations that viewed crossdressing and crossgender behavior as perverse and pathological prevailed (see Pauly, 1965, for a more detailed review). In the context of the sexual revolution, the Christine Jorgenson case and the work of Harry Benjamin helped shift the treatment pendulum from attempting to "cure" the transvestite or transsexual with psychoanalysis (see Kuiper, 1991, for a review) or aversion treatment (see Gelder & Marks, 1969, for a review) to facilitating acceptance and management of a gender role transition.

Benjamin's scale to determine the intensity of gender dysphoria became widely used by clinicians after 1966. When major psychopathology (e.g., schizophrenia, psychosis) could be ruled out, this scale was used to assess whether the client was a "true" transsexual and to guide treatment, including the indication for sex reassignment. Because of Benjamin's emphasis on the intensity of gender dysphoria, less severe comorbid psychopathology was likely to be ignored in the decisions regarding treatment and sex reassignment. Anxiety or depression was more likely to be seen as consequences of intense gender dysphoria which could be alleviated through sex reassignment. Hormonal and surgical sex reassignment became the option of choice to relieve the gender identity conflict of these "true" transsexuals. For many years, gender dysphoria clinics around the world used this scale as well as the Standards of Care for hormonal and surgical sex reassignment established by the Harry Benjamin International Gender Dysphoria Association (Walker, Berger, Green, Laub, Reynolds & Wollman, original draft 1979, revised drafts 1980, 1981 and 1990).

Thirteen years after Benjamin's work, a widely publicized study by Meyer and Reter (1979) indicated that sex reassignment did not decrease distress and suicide among transsexuals, or improve their life functioning. These results were used to support a decision in 1979 (Money, 1991a) to discontinue sex reassignment services at Johns Hopkins University (the first major center in the United States for sex reassignment surgeries) and prompted many health care professionals to reevaluate hormonal and surgical sex reassignment as the treatment of choice for transsexualism. In the United States, for example, Meyer and Reter's study was quickly used by health insurance companies to deny coverage for sex reassignment. While other follow-up studies arrived at very different and more positive conclusions (for reviews, see Green & Fleming, 1990, or Kuiper, 1991), whether or not to advocate hormonal and surgical sex reassignment has continued to be controversial. In the late 1970s and early 1980s, Lothstein and Levine began discussing the importance of recognizing cormorbid psychopathology in the assessment and treatment of gender dysphoric individuals (Lothstein, 1977; Levine, 1980; Levine & Lothstein, 1981; Lothstein & Levine, 1981). Their work is consistent with the current trend in clinical sexology to view symptoms and diagnoses in the context of an individual's overall mental and physical functioning. This trend is also reflected in the most recent edition of the Diagnostic and Statistical Manual (DSM-III-R) of the American Psychiatric Association (1987), in which the authors put greater emphasis on making a differential diagnosis and introducing a multi-axial diagnostic system and, thereby, acknowledging the multi-faceted nature of presenting complaints and mental disorders.

Today, more clinicians recognize that gender dysphoria is far more complex than previously assumed (Bradley, Blanchard, Coates, Green, Levine, Meyer-Bahlburg, Pauly, Zucker, 1991). There is no scientific consensus about a single developmental pathway which leads to gender dysphoria. Determinants of gender dysphoria remain controversial and hypothetical. Although some cases may offer support for Stoller's psychoanalytic etiological theory of "transsexualism" (Stoller, 1975), applicants for sex reassignment present with diverse backgrounds in terms of family dynamics and psychosexual development. While other theorists have posited a biological, deterministic view (e.g., Pillard & Weinrich, 1987), there is insufficient evidence for a biological determinant of gender dysphoria (Gooren, 1984, 1986a,b, 1987, 1991; Coleman, Gooren & Ross, 1989). Interactionist theories of psychosexual development (Money & Ehrhardt, 1972; Money, 1988) are more likely to represent reality.

A COMPREHENSIVE TREATMENT MODEL

The treatment model which we currently use reflects this complexity by integrating treatment of gender dysphoria into treatment of the overall mental health of the client. The treatment plan does not isolate the client's gender identity conflict but takes into account the client's total psychosociosexual adjustment, including comorbid psychiatric and other physical pathology. Our approach moves away from trying to distinguish the "true transsexual" (Benjamin, 1966) from the "nontranssexual applicant for sex reassignment" (e.g., Newman & Stoller, 1974; Stermac, 1990). Instead, we argue that a central purpose of treatment is to facilitate mental health and identity development.

Gender/sexual identity is only one aspect of overall identity. Addressing identity development from a general developmental (Erikson, 1956), interpersonal (Sullivan, 1953), and psychiatric perspective is critical in improving our clients' overall psychological functioning. Identity development is often hampered by primary comorbid psychopathology, usually stemming from early childhood. Therefore, we address these problems first and then work to foster identity development. Thus, our clients are treated with a variety of psycho- and pharmacotherapies. Sex reassignment may be recommended but only after identity development tasks have been addressed.

In our comprehensive treatment model, five treatment tasks can be distinguished: (1) Assessment; (2) Management of comorbid psychiatric disorders; (3) Facilitating identity formation (analysis of biography, family of origin intimacy dysfunction/abuse recovery, sexual identity exploration); (4) Sexual identity management (decision making, sexual functioning, social support); and (5) Aftercare. Figure 1 provides an overview of the treatment model and tasks.

TREATMENT TASKS

Assessment

As noted, this approach integrates treatment of gender dysphoria into treatment of the client's overall mental health. This requires a comprehensive evaluation to establish a well-justified differential diagnosis.

While many clients who present with gender dysphoria meet

Figure 1: COMPREHENSIVE TREATMENT MODEL

PSYCHOEDUCATION   Special Topic Lectures

I. ASSESSMENT
Clinical interviews (individual/couple/family)
Psychological testing
Physical examination
* Chemical dependency evaluation

Treatment Subtasks
A.   Analysis of biography
B.   Family of origin intimacy
     dysfunction/abuse recovery
C.   Sexual identity exploration

II. MANAGEMENT OF COMORBID DISORDERS
Psychotherapy
* Chemical dependency treatment
* Pharmacotherapy

III. FACILITATING IDENTITY FORMATION

Treatment Modalities
- Individual/couple/family psychotherapy   or
- Abuse Recovery Group
  Family therapy
- Sexual Orientation Conflict Group
  Gender Identity Therapy Group
  Gender Dysphoria Seminar

Compulsive
Sexual
Behavior
Therapy Group

IV. SEXUAL IDENTITY MANAGEMENT
Treatment Modalities
- Gender Identity Therapy Group
- Individual psychotherapy
- Individual/couple psychotherapy
  Sexual dysfunction therapy group
  Sexual Attitude Reassessment Seminar

- Couple/family/group psychotherapy

Treatment Subtasks
A.   Decision making
B.   Sexual functioning

C.   Social support

V. AFTERCARE
Gender Identity Consolidation Therapy Group
Individual/couple/family psychotherapy

* if indicated

DSM criteria for gender identity disorders, simply focusing on these disorders ignores the complexity of an individual's psychosexual and psychiatric history. This is particularly true for those who meet criteria for transsexualism. For many clients as well as professionals, this diagnosis presupposes sex reassignment as the treatment of choice. Implying sex reassignment early on precludes the exploration of cormorbid psychopathology and of the various dynamics and motivations for sex reassignment. This approach has potentially disastrous consequences given the irreversibility of hormonal and surgical sex reassignment.

In our experience, the gender dysphoric client's distress cannot be completely attributed to the perceived gender identity conflict or to a history of gender nonconformity. These are important factors, but disposition and life experiences relatively unrelated to gender also determine the client's current adjustment, and may contribute to the desire for sex reassignment. Sometimes the desire for sex reassignment is a cry for help, an expression of psychological pain stemming from a long history of anxious attachments, generalized anxiety, social phobia, intimacy dysfunction, depression, loneliness and despair. Consistent with previous research (see Lothstein, 1984, or Kuiper, 1991, for a review), we find that many clients suffer from a variety of Axis I disorders (most commonly anxiety and depressive disorders), as well as Axis II personality disorders. While Axis I disorders are often quite evident, prolonged contact with the client is usually required to confirm the presence of a personality disorder.

In terms of assessing the sexual identity conflicts, we have found existing classifications inadequate. We have already discussed the limitations of the Harry Benjamin Scale. Another popular classification system is the one developed by Blanchard (1987, 1989, 1990), which distinguishes homosexual from heterosexual or nonhomosexual gender dysphoria. This system has its limitations because of its attempt to reduce the wide spectrum of gender dysphoria into two main types, based upon the sexual orientation of the client. We have argued that this classification system overemphasizes the relevance of sexual orientation in understanding the client's gender identity and dysphoria (Coleman & Bockting, 1988; Bockting & Coleman, 1991; Coleman, Bockting & Gooren, 1993).

For the assessment of sexual identity, we have adapted the de-

scriptive model by Shively and DeCecco (1977). Shively and De-
Cecco distinguish among four components of sexual identity: biological sex, gender identity, social sex role and sexual orientation.
We use the term "natal sex" rather than "biological sex" to refer to
physical characteristics and gender at birth as suggested by Money
(1991b). We disagree with many theories of sexual and gender
identity development, which link these four components. For example, in gender transposition theories, a same-sex sexual orientation
implies a certain degree of crossgender identification. This theoretical framework implies a stereotypical view of the homosexual individual, one which extant research among large samples of homo-
sexually identified individuals (e.g., Bell & Weinberg, 1978) does
not support. Linkages between sexual orientation and gender identity also fail to be supported by biological and psychohormonal research on sexual differentiation (Coleman, Gooren, & Ross, 1989).
In spite of this evidence, childhood cross social-sex-role behavior,
such as a boy's preference to play with dolls, is often viewed incor-
rectly as an indication of crossgender identity. In gender dysphoric
individuals, the four components of sexual identity can be combined in a multitude of ways (Coleman, 1987a; Coleman, Bockting
& Gooren, 1993). Using Shively and DeCecco's model enables us
to differentiate between social sex role dysphoria (i.e., the client's
discomfort with society's sex role expectations or own sex role
nonconformity), sexual orientation dysphoria (i.e., the client's discomfort with same sex sexual attraction), and gender dysphoria.

The implication of this for the assessment of sexual identity is
that all four components must be assessed separately. This assessment cannot be made immediately but is revealed in the ongoing
process of psychotherapy. We have found that some clients maintain a scripted or pseudo-identity in the desire to present themselves
as an appropriate candidate for sex reassignment. Others define
themselves as conforming to traditional stereotypes which conflicts
with their past behavior and attractions. Still others are confused
and are simply not able to define themselves in terms of their sexual
identity. Hence, sexual identity is reassessed after psychotherapy
has facilitated further sexual identity development.

The evaluation of gender dysphoric clients at our clinic consists
of two one-hour interviews and the administration of a battery of

psychological tests, including the Minnesota Multiphasic Personality Inventory-II (Hathaway & McKinley, 1989), the Tennessee Self Concept Scale (Fitts, 1964), the Derogatis Sexual Functioning Inventory (Derogatis & Melisaratos, 1979), the Milcom Health History Questionnaire (Hollister, 1980), and the Assessment of Sexual Orientation (Coleman, 1987a). For gender dysphoric clients who are in a relationship, testing also includes the Sexual Interaction Inventory (LoPiccolo & Steger, 1974), the Dyadic Adjustment Scale (Spanier, 1976), and the Styles of Conflict Inventory (Metz, 1992). Among the areas covered in the clinical interviews are a complete psychological and psychiatric history, family and sexual history, and a history of intimate attachments. A physical examination is conducted for evidence of physical illness, including hormonal or chromosomal abnormalities. In cases where chemical abuse is suspected, an extensive chemical dependency evaluation is included. Following scoring of the tests, cases are discussed in a staff meeting consisting of a multi-disciplinary team of several psychologists, a family physician and a psychiatrist. A differential diagnosis is made and an individualized treatment plan addressing all aspects of the client's adjustment is developed. Previous treatment is taken into consideration. After the evaluation, the client meets with the assigned primary therapist and a treatment contract is established.

Management of Comorbid Disorders

If assessment uncovers comorbid disorders, their treatment is incorporated into the treatment plan. Symptoms of anxiety and depression form a barrier to engaging in psychotherapy. We have found the serotonergic anti-depressant fluoxetine (Prozac®) and the mood modulator lithium carbonate, extremely helpful in alleviating these symptoms. In addition to facilitating engagement in psychotherapy, these medications may decrease the intensity of the dysphoria, relieving what is often an obsession with obtaining hormonal and/or surgical sex reassignment. It is interesting to note that the same medication regimens have been found helpful in reducing obsessive and compulsive sexual behavior (Cesnik & Coleman, 1989; Coleman & Cesnik, 1990; Kafka, 1991, Coleman, Cesnik,

Moore, & Dwyer, 1992). We hypothesize that for some gender dysphoric clients, their crossdressing and crossgender feelings are the focus of their obsessive/compulsive behavior and a means of coping with anxiety.

Other professionals (e.g., Steiner, Satterberg, & Muir, 1978; Steiner, 1985; Stermac, 1990) report that providing hormones can significantly reduce or eliminate the urgent desire for surgical sex reassignment. Newman and Stoller (1974) also found that in some cases hormones in small dosages relieve the client's intense gender distress, however, they report that in other cases, hormones only increase the desire for surgery. We are cautious about treating the gender dysphoric client's despair due to comorbid psychopathology with sex hormones, and prefer to try other medications specifically developed for this purpose. We are concerned about how the client constructs his or her identity after being given "male" or "female" hormones. This may force a premature consolidation of a cross-gender identity and may intensify the desire for surgical sex reassignment (Morgan, 1978).

Facilitating Identity Formation

Analysis of Biography

Following assessment and management of anxiety, depressive, and substance abuse disorders that impair the client's ability to engage in psychotherapy, the client is assigned to write his or her biography. This biography includes, but is not limited to, a detailed sexual history. In analyzing the biography, we use a symbolic inter-actionist approach (Plummer, 1975, 1987), noting the meaning the individual assigns to past, present and future life experiences. We are less interested in what actually happened, and more interested in how the client structures his or her reality. Levine (1984) has also used this approach in understanding the dynamics of an individual's gender dysphoria. Through journaling and sharing the biography with others (therapist, group members, and sometimes family members and friends), meanings of past experiences are cognitively reconstructed. Suppressed feelings are reexamined. Barriers to healthy sexual identity development are identified and resolved.

The goal of this process is to help the client begin to move toward identity integration. Models of homosexual identity development reviewed and integrated by Minton and McDonald (1984) in a symbolic interactionist perspective, have been helpful to us in identifying the various developmental tasks involved in this process. Because both homosexuality and gender nonconformity are stigmatized in our culture, gender dysphoric individuals experience some of the same developmental hurdles as homosexual individuals (Coleman, 1981/82).

By working through his or her biography, the client and therapist can put gender dysphoria into a context of broader identity development. This is helpful in determining realistic therapeutic goals, and can clarify the potential of sex reassignment in the process of identity integration. Only after they have completed their biography and have addressed their family of origin issues, are clients encouraged to experiment with management of their sexual identity. Our therapeutic approach encourages clients to delay this exploration because it can distract from the important, difficult and often anxiety-provoking task of reviewing personal history.

The process of identity formation is fostered by individual psychotherapy, followed by group and family psychotherapy. Involving family members (both current family and family of origin) early in treatment is extremely helpful. Often the family helps put the client's gender dysphoric feelings in perspective of their psychosociosexual development. Family members may provide information that the client did not consider relevant, was unaware of, or held back in fear of rejection for sex reassignment.

Family of Origin Intimacy Dysfunction/Abuse Recovery

In reviewing the client's biography, evidence of family of origin intimacy dysfunction or childhood abuse may be encountered. In such cases, the effect on the client's identity development and ability to form intimate relationships is addressed. A number of relationships between an individual's abuse history and his or her gender dysphoria are possible. Some of these abusive experiences may relate directly to gender, for example the experience of being cross-dressed as a child by family members, and ridiculed as such. Other abusive experiences might appear unrelated to gender (e.g., verbal and emotional abuse by mother and neglect by father), however with further analysis appear to be reenacted in a metaphorical way through crossdressing and crossgender fantasies. Finally, other abusive experiences unrelated to gender may simply have affected the client's ability to cope with gender nonconformity or crossgender identification.

We have found a high incidence of childhood physical abuse, ridicule and emotional neglect among our clients. Early childhood trauma, dysfunctional family systems and dysfunctional family attitudes about sex and intimacy can create a number of psychological disorders (most commonly anxiety and personality disorders) which disrupt psychosocial and psychosexual development. Kohut (1977) has described how abused and neglected children are concerned with the very survival of the self. The child grows up with the feeling that relationships are dangerous. Kohut suggests that neurosis is a manifestation of a dread (anxiety) of disintegration of the self. This disintegration anxiety is caused by a weakened or damaged self image, which is usually a result of faulty interactions between the child's parental figures. This theory of self psychology suggests that the most urgent function of the coping mechanism is to restore or maintain the intactness of self (Stolorow & Lachmann, 1980). Individuals can use a wide variety of coping mechanisms to ward off disintegration anxiety. For many, these traumatic experiences provoke primary anxiety disorders.

For example, in clients whose gender dysphoria has increased after a history of fetishistic transvestism or sexual orientation dysphoria, we find that the crossdressing and gender dysphoria exhibit obsessive/compulsive features and serve as a way to cope with psychological pain originating from childhood abuse and family intimacy dysfunction. By obsessively ruminating about a desired gender, the individual avoids the pain of childhood memories. In some cases, the wish to make a role transition is an attempt to dissociate from the childhood experiences. Addressing family of origin intimacy dysfunction and childhood abuse in psychotherapy not only illuminates the meaning of the gender dysphoria, but also results in adopting new coping and intimacy skills that improve integration and identity management.

In our treatment program, family of origin intimacy dysfunction and childhood abuse are addressed in group psychotherapy. In cases of significant childhood abuse and continued patterns of victimization, participation in a short-term group for victims of childhood abuse (model described by Brown, 1991) is recommended. In cases where sexual behavior, crossdressing and gender dysphoria have become the focus of an obsessive/compulsive way of coping with anxiety, participation in a group for individuals with compulsive sexual behavior (model described by Coleman, 1987b; 1990; 1991; 1992) is recommended. Neither group consists solely of gender dysphoric clients, which prevents potential collusion around the crossdressing and gender dysphoria and helps the client stay focused on the treatment task. In addition, group psychotherapy provides a powerful experience of intimacy, the first of that kind for some gender dysphoric clients.

When indicated and feasible, clients may also personally confront family of origin members in family psychotherapy. This provides both client and family with an opportunity to resolve family of origin conflicts and improve intimacy functioning.

Sexual Identity Exploration

In the process of identity formation through reexperiencing and restructuring personal history, the client is encouraged to verbalize gender feelings and conflict. The client's cognitions are examined with an emphasis on the meaning of being male/female, man/ woman, masculine/feminine, and how this applies to himself or herself. Conflicts between the four components of sexual identity (natal sex, gender identity, social sex role and sexual orientation) are identified and explored. This helps clarify the sexual identity conflict for the client. In addition, the client is encouraged to experiment with living as a man/woman exploring masculine/feminine social sex roles, and to experience himself or herself in relationship with others (as males/females with various combinations of gender identities, social sex roles and sexual orientations).

In cases of a conflict between natal sex and sexual orientation, where gender dysphoria is secondary to sexual orientation dysphoria, participation in a therapy group for individuals with sexual orientation conflict (model described by Coleman, 1981/1982) is recommended. In cases of a conflict between natal sex and gender identity, participation in a therapy group for gender dysphoria (the Gender Identity Therapy Group) is recommended. This group provides the opportunity to identify with others who are in various stages of exploring their crossgender feelings.

Sexual Identity Management

Decision Making

As part of the ongoing process of identity formation and exploration, the client is encouraged to begin to make decisions about sexual identity. The role of the therapist is to facilitate a process in which clients discover the most effective way to manage their sexual identities. Like sexual identity exploration, sexual identity management is addressed in group psychotherapy. This provides the gender dysphoric client with the opportunity to identify with others who have chosen different options and are in various stages of identity management, including transition to a desired gender role.

Often gender dysphoric clients have a more ambiguous gender identity and are more ambivalent about a gender role transition than they initially admit. It is common for the client to seek assurance from the clinician through confirmation of a diagnosis of transsexualism (also acknowledged by Lothstein, 1977, Levine & Lothstein, 1981). Our treatment model challenges clients to review their motivations for solutions to their gender dysphoria and to think creatively regarding identity management. This allows gender dysphoric clients to discover and express their unique identity, as opposed to adopting a stereotypical one out of their intense need to conform.

A client's options in resolving the gender identity conflict range from integration of crossgender feelings in the role congruent with one's natal sex, to living part or full time in the role of the other sex without any medical interventions, to hormonal and/or surgical sex reassignment.

When the option of sex reassignment is chosen, hormonal and surgical sex reassignment are considered separately. We make no assumption that hormonal sex reassignment must be followed by surgical sex reassignment. Partial anatomical sex reassignment is a valid option in itself, and for many clients a more realistic one, given the expense of surgery. For example, many natal females with gender dysphoria are quite content with the removal of breast tissue and do not see the need for a hysterectomy, genito-, or phallo-plasty.

Physical changes are not supported until identity is sufficiently formed and integration has begun. The "real-life test" (Money & Ambinder, 1978) is initiated for clients to express their desired sexual identity as a means for further experimentation, reality testing and identity development (for a more elaborate discussion see Pauly, 1990). This "real-life test" is accompanied by ongoing psychotherapy which addresses overall adjustment, including building a social support system.

Realistically, many gender dysphoric clients must prepare to live as a "transsexual" or "transgenderist," because their ability "to pass" or not be recognized as such is limited.

Pragmatic concerns sometimes determine the option of choice. For example, one of our natal male gender dysphoric clients concluded that he felt neither man nor woman, identifying as gender neutral. He experimented with living as such, but quickly discovered that this was extremely difficult. The confusion this provoked for others made a gender neutral lifestyle extremely stressful. He decided to experiment with living as a woman, despite that this was not his internal self identification. He discovered that "playing a woman" was, in the present society, the best option for him. He experienced more freedom to express himself in the female gender role than in the more narrowly defined male gender role.

Other pragmatic issues regarding a decision for sex reassignment include feelings of partners, family and children, potential interference with career development, desire to maintain the option of switching gender roles, fear of anatomical interventions, medical health concerns and financial constraints. At all times, it is important to keep the option of sex reassignment open. Clients may decide to explore other options temporarily.

A unique aspect of our treatment model is that it allows for individuals to identify as neither man nor woman, but as someone whose identity transcends the culturally sanctioned dichotomy. For example, for some of our male gender dysphoric clients, identifying as a stereotypical heterosexual woman is not a desired goal because they cannot identify with the rigid gender schema of western culture. The model also gives those pursuing sex reassignment permission to be less rigid in their social sex role expression. After introduction of this model, one of our sex reassigned male-to-female transsexuals felt safe enough to share her discomfort with the effort involved in "passing" as a woman. She wished to present herself as "as is," and was able to realize that her appearance mattered less than how she felt inside.

While our decisions regarding sex reassignment are based on the Harry Benjamin Standards, we have additional requirements which involve pursuing the aforementioned treatment tasks.

In cases where hormonal and surgical sex reassignment are sought by the client, a decision to recommend reassignment is made by a Gender Committee, consisting of a multi-disciplinary team of psychologists, physicians and a psychiatrist. In addition to a case presentation by the primary therapist, the client is interviewed by the Committee. To protect the trust of the therapeutic relationship, the primary therapist does not vote in the decision process whether or not sex reassignment is recommended. This process helps the therapist stay in the role of an advocate for the client's self interest, rather than as a decision maker. It also limits the power of counter-transference issues as the Gender Committee can make a more unbiased and objective decision.

Sexual Functioning

When sexual and gender identity are sufficiently consolidated, the focus of therapy shifts to sexual functioning and enrichment. It is particularly difficult to encourage clients who are pursuing sex reassignment to work on this therapeutic task. However, addressing sexual health offers an excellent opportunity to demystify the surgical outcome for these gender dysphoric clients. For example, many natal female clients pursuing sex reassignment avoid touching their genitals, and do not allow genital stimulation in their sexual relationships. The client's task is to become realistic about the limitations of surgery, and to evaluate the relative significance of one's body and genital morphology.

For this treatment task, we use cognitive-behavioral approaches with which most sex therapists are familiar (Wincze & Carey, 1991; Halvorson & Metz, 1992). Clients explore their bodies at home through prescribed sexual exercises. These exercises include self-pleasuring and self-nurturing techniques that enhance self esteem. In cases of surgical sex reassignment, the sex therapy continues after surgery to help the clients adjust to body alterations. This task in treatment helps gender dysphoric clients become more comfortable with themselves and in social and intimate relationships, regardless of whether they undergo sex reassignment surgery. In some cases, addressing the genital sexual functioning brings to the surface remaining barriers to intimacy and identity integration.

Social Support

Often the gender dysphoric client is socially isolated, lacks the skills to access support or to cope with the difficulties of sexual identity integration. Such loneliness can contribute to the intensity of gender dysphoria. For the client to achieve an integrated identity, sources of social support must be made available. With the additional stigma of sex reassignment as a choice of identity management, the need for a social support system is magnified.

Intimacy skills are taught through the therapeutic relationship and through group and family psychotherapy. Clients pursuing sex reassignment often want to avoid their past and begin anew, but we encourage them to use their existing support as well as building new support systems. However, the family and old friends need help to adjust to the client's sexual identity. As with the homosexual identity coming out process (Coleman, 1981/82), the families and friends of gender dysphoric clients go through their own process of "coming out." The family therapy assists both the client and the family and friends in this process.

The same holds true for clients' relationships with their employers and coworkers. In some cases, we provide in-service training and consultation to employers and employees.

Aftercare

Treatment does not end with the client's decision regarding identity management. In our experience, clients often tend to reevaluate their decisions. Individuals who have chosen sex reassignment have often focused so long on gaining support for their decision that they experience anxiety about the surgery and grief over lost time once they gain approval for reassignment. As with cases where other options than sex reassignment are chosen, we provide supportive psychotherapy to consolidate the client's achieved identity.

When sex reassignment is chosen, reactions of family members and friends will often take a dramatic turn. Family members may have been in denial, thinking (or hoping) that their relative's gender dysphoria would pass. With impending or actual reassignment, emotions about such a significant change resurface. Families and friends who were previously accepting may suddenly end their support. As time passes, most family members and friends accept the gender dysphoric person's decision for reassignment. They also come to realize that withholding support to their family member will not change his or her mind about hormonal or surgical reassignment.

For those who are in the process of anatomical sex reassignment, the Gender Identity Consolidation Therapy Group provides continuing care and support in living in the acquired gender role. Fears and anxiety about the upcoming surgery or role transition are aired and the client is given support, practical information and therapeutic assistance. Many still have unrealistic expectations of what the surgery will involve or accomplish, and therapists can provide accurate information about the process.

PSYCHOEDUCATION

Throughout the course of treatment, psychoeducation is provided through monthly lectures and workshops, as well as two seminars. The monthly Special Topic Lectures address both topics related to gender and sexuality, and general mental health for the gender dysphoric client. Examples are lectures about assertiveness, childhood abuse, identity development, sex reassignment surgery, electrolysis and crosscultural crossgender behavior.

As soon as clients have begun the task of identity exploration, they participate in the Gender Dysphoria Seminar, a half-day workshop providing information on the wide spectrum of crossdressing and gender dysphoria. This workshop includes a panel of clients who have completed treatment. In addition to providing information, feelings, attitudes and values regarding gender nonconformity are discussed in small groups. Clients are encouraged to bring their partners, families and friends to the seminar.

As part of the treatment task of addressing sexual functioning, clients and their partners participate in the Sexual Attitude Reassessment Seminar (Lief, 1970). In this two-day seminar, a wide variety of sexual health issues are addressed, ranging from sexual development, sexual victimization, HIV/AIDS, other sexually transmitted diseases and safer sex, to sex roles, sexual orientation, intimacy and sexual communication.

CONCLUSION

In conclusion, we acknowledge that assessing the appropriateness of sex reassignment is a difficult task. Recognizing this, John Money designed the "real-life test" (Money & Ambinder, 1978), which requires an individual requesting sex reassignment surgery to live in the desired gender role for at least one year before surgery. However, we believe that this test alone is insufficient. An assessment of motivations and comorbid psychiatric disorders needs to precede the "real-life test." This must be followed by psychotherapy to uncover and resolve motivations which will not be addressed by sex reassignment. Other therapies treat comorbid psychiatric disorders, which might alleviate the gender dysphoria or reduce its intensity so that crossgender identity can be integrated into overall sexual identity. Treatment of the comorbid psychiatric disorders can also assist the individual seeking sex reassignment to better engage in and take advantage of therapy which will increase the chances of post-reassignment adjustment.

The comprehensive treatment model outlined in this paper has implications for classification and ethical standards of care for the treatment of gender dysphoria. Many of the clients who present with a desire for sex reassignment at our clinic, meet DSM III-R criteria for a diagnosis of transsexualism. Clients often have a dichotomous view of transsexualism and are seeking confirmation from a professional that they are a "true transsexual," which for many implies anatomical sex reassignment. But diagnosing the client at this point as transsexual is misleading to the client and can interfere with the therapeutic exploration of crossgender feelings in the context of the psychosociosexual history, working toward identity integration and making a rational decision about sex reassignment.

Contrary to the interim report of the DSM IV Subcommittee on Gender Identity Disorders (Bradley, Blanchard, Coates, Green, Levine, Meyer-Bahlburg, Pauly, & Zucker, 1991), we suggest that future revisions of the DSM stop defining gender identity disorders in relation to a person's sexual orientation. We have not found this a useful distinction in the assessment of gender dysphoria and find it an unnecessary distraction. Further, this distinction has been used to discriminate against natal female gender dysphoric individuals who might be candidates for reassignment but who are attracted to men (defined as "heterosexual" by DSM III–but who identified as "homosexual" following reassignment) (Coleman & Bockting, 1988; Coleman, Bockting & Gooren, 1993). Our treatment model advocates a clear separation of gender identity, social sex role and sexual orientation, which allows a wide spectrum of sexual identities and prevents limiting access to sex reassignment services to those who conform to a heterosexist paradigm of mental health.

We advocate restricting the term "transsexual" to those who have undergone a gender role transition, including anatomical changes. Gender identity disorders do have a place in classification systems of disorders, as many individuals engaging in crossdressing and crossgender behavior present with significant distress and impairment in psychosociosexual functioning associated with their gender nonconformity. A dynamic and phenomenological understanding of gender identity conflict is necessary to alleviate this distress. But given the current lack of consensus about the etiology of gender dysphoria, it seems appropriate for DSM to limit itself to a descriptive classification system allowing for the diverse clinical presentations of gender dysphoria. The classification of gender identity disorder in itself should not imply a prescribed solution.

In addition, we have emphasized the need for differential diagnoses, in which dual axis I diagnoses of gender identity disorder and generalized anxiety disorder, dysthymia and obsessive/compulsive disorder are common.

The model outlined in this paper uses the Harry Benjamin International Standards of Care for the hormonal and surgical sex reassignment of gender dysphoric persons as minimal criteria for supporting client's decisions to undergo hormonal and/or surgical sex reassignment. In our treatment approach, these standards alone are insufficient for our Gender Committee to grant approval for hormonal and/or surgical sex reassignment. It should be noted that the Standards of Care were meant to be *minimal* standards. Therefore, our criteria for reassignment are not inconsistent with the intent of the Standards of Care. Our prerequisites reflect our philosophy that comorbid disorders must be managed adequately, that treatment tasks be accomplished and that a certain level of identity integration needs to be achieved before the initiation of anatomical changes through hormones and surgery.

The current Standards of Care allow for hormone therapy to be initiated after evaluation and a three-month therapeutic relationship with a specialized provider. In our opinion, this is not long enough for the treatment tasks we have outlined. In the United States, the financial resources of many gender dysphoric clients limit the frequency of psychotherapy. In three months, not much more can be expected than establishing a therapeutic relationship as a prerequisite to the necessary psychotherapy. Again, many clients who present with a desire for sex reassignment are in crisis and often are obsessively focused on sex reassignment. We recommend a minimum of six months of ongoing psychotherapy before the onset of hormone therapy. Finally, we suggest that the Standards of Care include guidelines to ensure that the gender dysphoric client has reached a level of psychological adjustment and identity integration, which includes having access to adequate social support, before decisions about identity management are made.

Ideally, we feel the gender dysphoric population can best be served through enrollment in a comprehensive program, with a multidisciplinary staff which offers medical, psychiatric, psychological and sociocultural perspectives. Within this comprehensive program, ongoing clinical research and education are needed to continue to increase our understanding of this complicated phenomenon and to improve client care. Providers who work with this population in private practice may encounter difficulties given the crisis-oriented nature of the clientele, the manipulation frequently involved, as well as the ethical and emotional dilemmas resulting from a decision regarding sex reassignment. To avoid these problems, professionals are encouraged to coordinate their treatment with specialists that can provide the necessary comprehensive assessment and treatment.

REFERENCES

American Psychiatric Association (1987). Diagnostic and Statistical Manual of Mental Disorders (3rd ed., rev.). Washington, DC: American Psychiatric Association.

Bell, A. & Weinberg, M. (1978). *Homosexualities: A study of diversity among men and women.* New York: Simon & Schuster.

Benjamin, H. (1966). *The transsexual phenomenon.* New York: The Julian Press, Inc.

Blanchard, R. (1987). Typology of male-to-female transsexualism. *Archives of Sexual Behavior, 14*(3), 247-261.

Blanchard, R. (1989). The classification and labeling of nonhomosexual gender dysphorias. *Archives of Sexual Behavior, 18*(4), 315-334.

Blanchard, R. (1990). Gender identity disorders in adult men. In R. Blanchard & B.W. Steiner (Eds.) *Clinical management of gender identity disorders in children and adults.* Washington DC, London, England: American Psychiatric Press, Inc.

Bockting, W.O. & Coleman, E. (1991). A comment on the concept of transhomosexuality, or the dissociation of the meaning. Letter to the editor. *Archives of Sexual Behavior, 20*(4), 419-421.

Bradley, S., Blanchard, R., Coates, S., Green, R., Levine, S., Meyer-Bahlburg, H.F.L., Pauly, I. & Zucker, K, (1991). Interim Report of the DSM-IV Subcommittee on Gender Identity Disorders. *Archives of Sexual Behavior, 20*(4), 333-343.

Brown, J. (1991). The treatment of male victims with mixed gender, short-term group psychotherapy. In M. Hunter (Ed.) *The Sexually Abused Male.* Lexington, MA: Lexington Books.

Cesnik, J.A. & Coleman, E. (1989). Use of lithium carbonate in the treatment of autoerotic asphyxia. *American Journal of Psychotherapy, 43*(2), 277-286.

Coleman, E. (1981/1982). Developmental stages of the coming out process. *Journal of Homosexuality,* 31-43.

Coleman, E. (1987a). Assessment of sexual orientation. *Journal of Homosexuality, 14*(1/2), 9-24.

Coleman, E. (1987b). Sexual compulsivity: Definition, etiology, and treatment considerations. In E. Coleman (Ed.) *Chemical Dependency and Intimacy Dysfunction.* New York: The Haworth Press, Inc.

Coleman, E. (1990). The obsessive-compulsive model for describing compulsive sexual behavior. *American Journal of Preventive Psychiatry & Neurology,* 2(3), 9-14.

Coleman, E. (1991). Compulsive sexual behavior: New concepts and treatment. *Journal of Psychology and Human Sexuality, 4*(2), 37-52.

Coleman, E. (1992). Is your patient suffering from compulsive sexual behavior? *Psychiatric Annals, 22*(6), 320-325.

Coleman, E. & Bockting, W. O. (1988). "Heterosexual" prior to sex reassignment, "homosexual" afterwards: A case study of a female-to-male transsexual. *Journal of Psychology and Human Sexuality, 1*(2), 69-82.

Coleman, E., Bockting, W.O, & Gooren, L.J.G. (1993). Homosexual and bisexual identity in sex reassigned female-to-male transsexuals. *Archives of Sexual Behavior, 22*(1).

Coleman, E. & Cesnik, J. (1990). Skoptic syndrome: The treatment of an obsessional gender dysphoria with lithium carbonate and psychotherapy. *American Journal of Psychotherapy, 44*(2), 204-217.

Coleman, E., Cesnik, J., Moore, A. & Dwyer, S.M. (1992). Exploratory study of the role of psychotropic medications in the psychological treatment of sex offenders. In E. Coleman & S.M. Dwyer (Eds.) Sex Offender Treatment: Psychological and Medical Approaches. New York: The Haworth Press, Inc.

Coleman, E., Gooren, L. & Ross, M. (1989). Theories of gender transpositions: A critique and suggestions for further research. *The Journal of Sex Research, 26*(4), 525-538.

Derogatis, L.R. & Melisaratos, N. (1979). The DSFI: a multidimensional measure of sexual functioning. *Journal of Sex and Marital Therapy, 5,* 244-81.

Docter, R.F. (1988). *Transvestites and Transsexuals: Toward a Theory of Cross-Gender Behavior.* New York and London: Plenum Press.

Erikson, E.H. (1956). The problem of ego identity. *Journal of the American Psychoanalytic Association, 4,* 56-121.

Fitts, W.H. (1964). Tennessee Self-Concept Scale. Western Psychological Services. Los Angeles, CA.

Gelder, M.G. & Marks, I.M. (1969). Aversion Treatment in Transvestism and Transsexualism. In R. Green & J. Money, (Eds.) *Transsexualism and Sex Reassignment.* Baltimore, Maryland: The Johns Hopkins Press.

Gooren, L.J.G. (1984). The naloxone-induced LH release in male-to-female transsexuals. *Neuroendocrinology.* Letter, *6,* 89-93.

Gooren, L.J.G. (1986a). The neuroendocrine response of luteinizing hormone to estrogen administration in the human is not sex specific but dependent on the hormonal environment. *Journal of Clinical Endocrinology and Metabolism, 83,* 589-593.

Gooren, L.J.G. (1986b). The neuroendocrine response of luteinizing hormone to estrogen administration in heterosexual, homosexual and transsexual subjects. *Journal of Clinical Endocrinology and Metabolism, 68,* 583-588.

Gooren, L.J.G. (1987). Reversal of the LH response to estrogen administration after orchidectomy in a male subject with androgen insensitivity syndrome. *Hormonal Versus Metabolic Research, 19,* 138.

Gooren, L.J.G. (1991). What do we know about the biology of gender dysphoria? "Meet the experts" presentation at the 10th World Congress for Sexology. Amsterdam, The Netherlands, June 20.

Green, R. & Fleming, D. (1990). Transsexual Surgery Follow-Up: Status in the 1990s. *Annual Review of Sex Research, 1,* 163-174.

Halvorsen, J.G. & Metz, M.D. (1992). Sexual Dysfunction, Part II, Diagnosis, Management and Prognosis, *Journal of the American Board of Family Practice, 5*(2), 177-192.

Hamburger, C., Sturup, C.K. & Dahl-Iversen, E. (1953). Transvestism, hormonal, psychiatric and surgical treatment. *Journal of the American Medical Association, 12*(6), 391-394.

Hathaway, S.A. & McKinley, J.C. (1989). Minnesota Multiphasic Personality Inventory. Minneapolis: The University of Minnesota Press.

Hollister. (1980). Milcom Health History Questionnaire.

Kafka, M. (1991). Successful antidepressant treatment of nonparaphilic sexual addictions and paraphilias in males. *Journal of Clinical Psychiatry, 52*(2), 60-65.

Kohut, H. (1977). *The Restoration of Self.* New York: International University Press.

Kuiper, A.J. (1991). *Transseksualiteit: Evaluatie van de geslachtsaanpassende behandeling.* Vrije Universiteit te Amsterdam, The Netherlands.

Levine, S.B. (1980). Psychiatric diagnosis of patients requesting sex reassignment surgery. *Journal of Sex & Marital Therapy, 6*:3, 164-173.

Levine, S.B. (1984). Letter to the Editor, *Archives of Sexual Behavior, 13*(3), 287-289.

Levine, S.B. & Lothstein, L. (1981). Transsexualism or the Gender Dysphoria Syndromes. *Journal of Sex and Marital Therapy, 7*(2), 85-113.

Lief, H.I. (1970). Developments in the Sex Education of the Physician. *Journal of the American Medical Association, 212,* 1864-1867.

LoPiccolo, J. & Steger, J.C. (1974). The sexual interaction inventory: a new instrument for assessment of sexual dysfunction. *Archives of Sexual Behavior, 3,* 585-95.

Lothstein, L.M. (1977). Psychotherapy with Patients with Gender Dysphoria Syndromes. *Bulletin of the Menninger Clinic, 41*(6), 563-583.

Lothstein, L.M. (1984). Psychological testing with transsexuals: a 30-year review. *Journal of Personality Assessment, 18,* 500-507.

Lothstein, L.M. & Levine, S.B. (1981). Expressive psychotherapy with gender dysphoric patients. *Archives of General Psychiatry, 38,* 924-929.

Metz, M.E. (1992). *The Styles of Conflict Inventory (SCI).* Palo Alto: Consulting Psychologist Press.

Meyer, J.K. & Reter, D.J. (1979). Sex reassignment follow-up. *Archives of General Psychiatry, 36*, 1010-1015.

Minton, H.L. & McDonald, G.J. (1984). Homosexual identity formation as a developmental process. *Journal of Homosexuality, 9*(2/3), 91-104.

Money, J. (1988). *Gay, Straight, and In-Between*. New York: Oxford Press.

Money, J. (1990). Serendipities on the Sexological Pathway to Research in Gender Identity and Sex Reassignment. *Journal of Psychology & Human Sexuality, 4*(1), 113.

Money, J. (1991a). Serendipities on the Sexological Pathway to Research in Gender Identity and Sex Reassignment. *Journal of Psychology & Human Sexuality, 4*(1), 101-113.

Money, J. (1991b). Nosological Sexology: A Prolegomenon. *Journal of Psychology & Human Sexuality, 4*(4), 111-120.

Money, J. & Ambinder, R. (1978). Two-year, real life diagnostic test: Rehabilitation versus cure. In J.P. Brady & H.K.H. Brodie (Eds.) *Controversy in Psychiatry*, Philadelphia: W.B. Saunders.

Money, J. & Ehrhardt, A.A. (1972). *Man & Woman, Boy & Girl: Differentiation and Dimorphism of Gender Identity from Conception to Maturity*. Baltimore: The Johns Hopkins Press.

Morgan, A.J. (1978). Psychotherapy for transsexual candidates screened out of surgery. *Archives of Sexual Behavior, 2*(4), 273-283.

Newman, L.E. & Stoller, R.J. (1974). Nontranssexual men who seek sex reassignment. *American Journal of Psychiatry, 131*(4), 437-441.

Pauly, I.B. (1965). Male psychosexual inversion: transsexualism: a review of 100 cases. *Archives of General Psychiatry, 13*, 172-181.

Pauly, I.B. (1990). Gender Identity Disorders: Evaluation and Treatment. *Journal of Sex Education & Therapy, 16*(1), 2-24.

Pillard, R.C. & Weinrich, J.D. (1987). The periodic table of the gender transpositions: A theory based on masculinization and feminization of the brain. *Journal of Sex Research, 23*(4), 425-454.

Plummer, K. (1975). *Sexual stigma: An interactionist account*. London: Routledge & Kegan Paul.

Plummer, K. (1987). Beyond childhood: organizing 'gayness' in adult life. Workshop, International conference "Homosexuality Beyond Disease," Amsterdam, The Netherlands.

Shively, M.G. & DeCecco, J.P. (1977). Components of Sexual Identity. *Journal of Homosexuality, 3*(1).

Spanier, G.B. (1976). Measuring dyadic adjustment: new scales for assessing the quality of marriage and similar dyads. *Journal of Marriage & Family, 38*, 15-28.

Steiner, B.W. (1985). The management of patients with gender disorders, in *Gender Dysphoria: Development, Research, Management*, B.W. Steiner (Ed.) New York: Plenum, 325-350.

Steiner, B.W., Satterberg, J.A. & Muir, C.F. (1978). Flight into femininity: the male menopause? *Canadian Psychiatric Association Journal, 23*, 405-410.

Stermac, L. (1990). Clinical management of nontranssexual patients. In R. Blanchard & B.W. Steiner (Eds.) *Clinical management of gender identity disorders in children and adults,* 107-118.

Stoller, R.J. (1975). *Sex & Gender. Volume II: The Transsexual Experiment.* New York: Jason Aronson .

Stolorow, R.D. & Lachman, F.M. (1980). Psychoanalysis of Developmental Arrests: Theory and Treatment. New York, International University Press, 50.

Sullivan, H.S. (1953). *The Interpersonal Theory of Psychiatry,* New York: Norton.

Walker, P., Berger, J., Green, R., Laub, D., Reynolds, C. & Wollman, L. (original draft 1979, revisions 1980, 1981, 1990). Standards of care: the hormonal and surgical sex reassignment of gender dysphoric persons. Palo Alto: The Harry Benjamin International Gender Dysphoria Association, Inc.

Wincze, J.P. & Carey, M.P. (1991). *Sexual Dysfunction: A Guide for Assessment and Treatment,* New York: The Guilford Press.